THE HISTORY O

and the surrounding area

ISBN: 0-9542137-0-X

Published by Portico Gallery
17b Upper Colqhoun Street
Helensburgh G84 9AJ
Tel: 01436 671821
Fax: 01436 677553
www.portico-gallery.com from whom supplies of this book may be
obtained

Produced with the assistance of
Librario Ltd
14 Harrow Inn Close
Elgin IV30 1BP
Tel. +44 (0) 1343 550 245
Fax. +44 (0) 1343 550 781

Printed and bound by Antony Rowe Ltd, Eastbourne

The History of Helensburgh

and the surrounding area

John B. Ashworth

Preface

During 28 years living in Helensburgh I have developed an interest in local matters and have had the opportunity to read many of the books mentioned in my bibliography (page 163). They are full of detailed material, but many of the items of interest are scattered widely. I have come to the conclusion that they are best brought to light in an easy-reading chronological format.

This is not intended to be a definitive book on any of the areas, except perhaps Helensburgh, as many in-depth books have been written about each area, and are readily available to more serious students.

The time-scale we are covering starts at the beginning of the first millennium and brings us to the present day. The title 'Helensburgh and the surrounding areas' is appropriate, as the town itself is a relatively recent development and a lot of the history of the area took place before its foundation and in the areas surrounding it.

The lower Clyde estuary is, broadly speaking, the arena for this book. The areas described embrace Loch Lomond, Dumbarton, Luss, Arrochar, Greenock, Gourock, Port Glasgow, Rosneath Peninsular, Garelochhead and Helensburgh, the hub of the area. The book seeks to link events over time throughout these parts.

I hope the reader will find some areas of interest in this book and will follow up with some in-depth reading from the source books identified in the bibliography, which in itself provides a list of the many books available to the avid reader in Helensburgh Library.

John B. Ashworth, O.B.E.
Helensburgh April 2001

CONTENTS

LIST OF ILLUSTRATIONS

The cover picture is reproduced by kind permission of M-Sat Ltd, Slough, Berks. It is a section of a satellite photograph taken from a height of 705 kilometres at a speed of 27,000 kilometres per hour.

1. Artist's impression of Malig – later Helensburgh – in 1770

Loch Lomond

Old Luss Road

Drumfork House

Route of Sinclair Street

Hermitage Park

Millig Mill

Site of Victoria Halls

Site of Colquhoun Square

Drumfork Ferry

East Bay

Millig Burn

Granary

Site of Pier

Glennan Burn

Site of Augusta Lodge

Site of Kidston Park

Ardencaple Castle

Cairndhu Inn

Chapter 1   AD 0 – 1000

Physical Environment – Roman Occupation – Antonines Wall –
Kingdom of Strathclyde.

It is worth reminding the reader of the environment in the area at the beginning of the first millennium. There were no roads or railways bordering on the riverbanks nor indeed ed any lights to penetrate the dusk. The area was substantially wooded down to the water's edge and would have appeared as a dark and desolate place.

The Clyde Estuary carried down the waters of the upper Clyde and the Leven, which were two shallow salmon streams which linked into the tidal estuary of the Clyde, below what is currently Dumbarton. The water levels came much higher up the land in in those days and this is demonstrated by the sea caves found in many areas – such as alongside the present Cardross village, Ardmore Point and below what was Ardencaple Castle.

There is further proof of the higher water level in the sand and shingle beds which can be found in the present Helensburgh as far as Colquhoun Square, and on the other side of the estuary up to Greenock town hall.

The 650 feet deep gorge that accommodates Loch Lomond was gouged out during a previous ice age. When the ice retreated the gorge filled with seawater, according to recent findings, between 5,300 and 3,500 b.c. For 800 years after the incursion period there was a salt-water layer in the loch.

One reason for water being so much higher was that the land was still recovering from the pressure of the ice age and was slowly rising to the level which the reader will see today. Dumbarton Rock was most of the time an island and the River Leven was tidal almost up to Loch Lomond.

The level of Loch Lomond was significantly lower than it is today. Over time the Vale of Leven has risen through gradual silting up to raise the level of the loch. At the beginning of the first millennium many of the islands in Loch Lomond around the Luss area were joined together and formed one chain of land. The building of the barrage across the River Leven in 1971 again caused the surface of the loch to rise to a higher level and many traces of civilisation, which were swallowed up by the rising of the loch, can be seen beneath the water.

The area was a perilous place before the beginning of the first millennium. Wolves, wild cats and other dangerous animals roamed the extensive forests. Small forest tracks were followed by groups of humans, though little is known about the local residents, except that they appear originally to have been bronze age man. The stones with ring and cup carvings on the hilltops at Milton and the ridge behind Helensburgh are evidence of their existence.

When the Romans arrived in AD 80 they referred to their battles with the Caledonii 'men of the woods'. As they progressively moved north within the British Isles, the Romans identified 31 distinct tribes. The ones in our area of interest were later designated the Picts, Scots and Attacotti.

The Attacotti tribe resisted the Romans long after the surrounding lands had been subdued and it is recorded that their area of influence was from Loch Fyne in the west across to Loch Lomond in the east and to the Antonine wall in the south. The Attacotti are thought to have indulged in atrocities peculiar to themselves. When they hunted for prey in the woods 'they attacked the shepherd as readily as the flock and selected with great care the most delicate and brawny parts of his body for their horrid repast'.

By AD 83 the Romans had built a series of forts from the Clyde to the Forth, but at that time there was no wall and much skirmishing between the invaders and the local tribes took place. This culminated in a great battle at the foot of the Grampians where the Roman, Galgacus, drove the tribes north and defeated an army of thirty thousand men.

By AD 117 the tribes were making many incursions into Roman

territory and shortly thereafter the Romans withdrew to Hadrians Wall to consolidate their position. In AD 137 Roman Governor Urbicus returned and created a wall across Scotland from Old Kilpatrick to the Firth of Forth, linking a line of Roman forts. He named it the Antonine wall, after Antonine Pius a senior Roman Senator. It was protected by a ditch, on its northern side, 20 feet deep and 40 feet wide which could be flooded in certain areas. The wall ended at the fort at Old Kilpatrick, although further forts at Dunglas and Dumbarton were part of the same defence mechanism. From there the Roman legions covered the river bank as a means of protecting the fords across the Clyde at Old Kilpatrick and Dumbuck. This was the lowest point of the Firth of Clyde capable of being forded. Indeed, it was recorded in 1769 that it was still only two feet deep at ebb tide.

From the death of Antonius in AD 161 there followed twenty years of turmoil with the tribes breaking through and laying waste to lands as far south as Hadrians Wall and beyond. Towards the close of the reign of Severus, in AD 209, decisive measures were taken to dispel the hostile tribes. Severus penetrated as far north as the Moray Firth and then made peace with the Caledonians who conceded the lands up to the Antonine wall to the Romans. No sooner had Severus withdrawn than the Caledonians re-engaged in hostility. Shortly afterwards, the new Emperor Caracalla became tired of warfare, made peace with the Caledonians and ceded the territory between the walls to them.

In AD 288, Carausius assumed the position of Roman leader in Britain and defended the original Roman boundaries, including the Antonius Wall, so successfully that for 80 years after his death they still ruled within those districts. By AD 367 the tribes again took up arms against the Romans and the Britons attacked southwards through Britain. Theodosius was sent to drive the tribes northwards beyond the Antonius wall again, creating Valencia between the Antonine and Hadrians Walls.

By AD 446 the Romans reviewed their territorial ambitions and sought to retreat and withdraw their soldiers. Governor Aetius urged self-government on the native tribes, of which there were two types, those living within the area known as Valencia and those living outside or to the north of the walls. They were much given to fighting and creating unrest, whilst those in Valencia were civilised by the Roman influence and capable of improvement.

At this time within the tribes to the north, their naked bodies were decorated with tattoos in the form of animals, and in battle they covered themselves with the blood of their slaughtered opponents. With the withdrawal of the Romans the era entered a dark and perplexing period with few factual records. Eventually the Romanised descendants of tribes occupying Valencia began to come together for mutual protection, leaving a portion of the east beyond the Lothians to the Picts. They formed on the west side a kingdom called Strathclyde whose boundaries were the Solway Firth in the south, the upper Forth and Loch Lomond in the north. The Scots who had emerged from Ireland held sway in Ayrshire and Argyll.

The first chief amongst the Britons of Strathclyde was Caunus who was soon in disagreement with the Picts. In battle they chased him out of the region and he took refuge in North Wales where an affinity between the peoples of that part of the world and Strathclyde was developing strongly. His son Hoel succeeded him and managed to attract the hostility of his uncle, Prince Arthur of Wales, with whom Caunus had taken refuge. When Hoel went to Anglesey, he was killed on the orders of Arthur who appears to have taken over the Kingdom of Strathclyde and added it to what was developing as the Kingdom of the Britons.

The Picts and Scots continued to harass the Britons of Strathclyde. In one battle, when Arthur marched up to Alcluid ("the rock of the Clyde" as Dumbarton was then known), the Picts and Scots retreated to Loch Lomond where there were 60 islands, 'full of eagles who flock there every year to nest, and make a loud noise'. Arthur obtained boats and sailed to besiege the enemy for 15 days, after which time "they were so straightened with hunger that they died in their thousands".

Whilst Arthur was harassing the Picts and Scots on the islands of Loch Lomond, Guillamurius, the king of Ireland, sailed up the Clyde with a fleet and army of barbarians in order to relieve the besieged. Arthur engaged and slew them without mercy, after which he proceeded with his first attempt to eliminate the Scots and Picts. After a short period the bishops of these peoples came barefoot bearing their religious relics. After pleading with King Arthur for mercy, they were pardoned.

King Arthur, killed by his nephew Medrawd, was buried in Glastonbury Abbey and succeeded in Strathclyde by Marken.

There was a succession of Kings of Strathclyde but relatively few records were kept until Domnal, who in AD 681 fought with several Irish tribes which had invaded Ayrshire. In the reign of the next King, Bile McElbhin, two battles took place in AD 710 and 720 between the Britons and the Scoto-Irish, who had settled in Argyllshire. The Britons were defeated on each occasion.

During this prolonged period of troubles, the Britons of Strathclyde enjoyed a few periods of peace between campaigns against their enemies. Having limited means of replacing their losses, it became apparent that this remarkable people, who for 300 years had remained independent in the midst of active enemies, were to succumb to repeated efforts to drive them out of their kingdom.

In 744 and 749 they again sustained attacks from their old enemies, the Picts. In 756 the Saxons and the Picts attacked the Britons with great determination and succeeded in penetrating Alclued which they partially destroyed. But the Britons were later amply revenged when they marched victorious to the very centre of their enemies' kingdom when they helped the Scottish Kings. This action prepared the way for the extinction of the Pictish monarchy which was effected by King Kenneth the Second in 843.

About this time the relationship between the Britons of Strathclyde and the Scots of Dalriada (Argyllshire) were of a more friendly nature, and inter-marriage took place between the two ruling families. This led to disagreement over the rights of leadership of Strathclyde, and the Scots declared war against the Strathclyde Prince named Artga in 871. As a result Alcluid (Dumbarton) was largely destroyed.

It was at this time that the Britons faced up to their most terrible enemy – the Vikings or Danish Sea Kings. Having created a settlement on the shores of Ireland, these fearsome warriors soon found their way across the Irish Sea and laid waste to the fertile valley of the Clyde.

In 870 the Vikings made the earliest recorded siege of the Castle of Dumbarton. The blockade commenced in the early part of the year. It continued for four months, until the defenders of the fort submitted when hunger, pestilence and repeated attacks weakened them so much that defence was impossible. After having plundered Alcluid of all that was valuable, the Danes spread over the surrounding country and subjected it to twelve months oppression. They returned four years later when they secured everything in and around Alcluid that had been spared in former ravages and destroyed what they could not carry off. They left the Britons of Strathclyde in the worst of all possible conditions – pillaged by the Danes, dictated to by the Scots and harassed by internal dissension. Their misfortunes were complete when they agreed, along with others, to the supremacy of the Anglo Saxons. Edward was chosen as King of Scots and also King of all the Strathclyde Britons.

From this period the history of the Kingdom of Strathclyde became more obscure and also less interesting. Hemmed in by enemies as unscrupulous as they were powerful, the people of Strathclyde became more unfit to contend with the success of these foes. The enfeebled Britons of Strathclyde made a last gallant struggle for independence, but the superior power of the Scots prevailed and they became masters of the whole territory of Strathclyde which was annexed to the dominion of the Scottish King.

The early history of the race by whom the Britons were subdued is worth recording. The Scots were emigrants from Ireland in the AD 500's and not natives of Britain. Although no longer governed by their native Princes, the Britons of Strathclyde continued for many centuries to inhabit the territory they originally possessed. Their language and customs remained the same, but the history of the Britons became so interwoven with that of the Scots that it is only events occurring amongst the latter which shed light on the conditions of ancient Dunbartonshire.

Whilst the records are very scarce, it seems that the natives of Strathclyde had progressed in their industry and references are made to the practice of agriculture in the era extending from the 400's to the 900's ad. The tending of sheep was a task assigned to St Patrick in his captivity. There is also reference to a barn which implies the practice of storing grain. In the Irish Annals for the year 650 there is mention of a bake house and mill; ploughing and sowing, and an abundant harvest. In addition, herbs and pulse and honey appear to form part of their diet. Orchards were plentiful in Strathclyde at one time, but their cultivation was often neglected in the civil commotions which disturbed the Kingdom.

In building, the use of stone seems to have been almost unknown, and dwelling houses and churches were built of rough timber, bound together by slender withes. Keeping up the means of communications within Strathclyde, the Britons appear to have continued with the example set by their Roman predecessors in navigation. Primitive canoes were generally giving place to "currachs", built from wicker frames, covered with skins of animals. They had mast, sails and oars, and it was in vessels like these that the local trading with the Western Isles and also the Missionaries' expeditions were conducted. St. Columba and St Cormack appeared to have performed lengthy and even dangerous voyages in them.

During the life of the Strathclyde kingdom the progress of Christianity was substantial. During five centuries, Kings and subjects alike appear to have contributed to the advance of that cause. Almost contemporary with St Patrick was Ninian who had laboured amongst the Britons of Strathclyde during the years 400 AD. He was described as a reverend Bishop and holy man of the British nation, who had regularly been instructed in Rome in the faith and mysteries of the truth. More closely connected with Dunbartonshire than even Ninian was Kentigern, who appeared among the Britons of Strathclyde in the 500's AD. It was said he was the illegitimate son of Eugene, the third King of Scots. Kentigern fixed his residence at Alcluid. Later, the jealous King, thinking the power of Kentigern clashed with his own, attempted to put an end to his career by imprisoning him, but he escaped to Wales, where he remained until he was recalled by the Kings of Strathclyde.

Kentigern then recommended his scheme of consolidating the ecclesicatical powers within Strathclyde. He accomplished this by becoming the founder of the diocese of Glasgow and the patron saint of the City. His last words were: "Glasgow should flourish by the preaching of the word". Thus Glasgow was founded on the basis of a religious settlement, central to the region of Strathclyde. Its commercial development followed from these small beginnings.

Chapter 2   *AD 1000 – 1250*

Kings of Strathclyde – Earldom of Lennox – Dumbarton Charters

In 1018, when Erwin King of Strathclyde was killed, Malcolm, the 2nd king of Alpan (formed by a merger of the Picts and Scots in 843), appointed his grandson Duncan to the kingship of Strathclyde which, on Malcolm's death in 1034, became amalgamated into the larger Scottish kingdom.

In 1072 William the Conqueror marched an army northward with the purpose of compelling Malcolm the 3rd to do homage for the possessions he held in England. Before hostilities broke out the two kings met in conference and Malcolm, the weaker of the two, submitted to the William's demands. But the Conqueror, not satisfied with Malcolm's promise or even the possession of his son Duncan as a hostage, laid waste in Northumberland and Cumberland and exterminated many of those families who favoured the Scottish monarch.

It is to this dim, disturbed period that genealogists trace the rise of the great house of Lennox. Among the Saxon chiefs of Northumbria, who fled for refuge to the court of Malcolm, was Arkil, the son of Egfrith, who in consideration for the noble stand he had made against the Conqueror, and as some recompense for the losses he sustained, received the gift of that tract of country described most frequently as "comitis de levenax". As the grant was made at a time when boundaries were not observed with a great strictness, it is difficult to indicate the exact extent of the estates, but it may be set down as containing at least what afterwards came to be known as the county of Dumbarton.

Though the title of Earl is supposed to be Coeval in antiquity, and equates with Thane, so well known in the north, it is uncertain when it was first used in Scotland: but Arkil's son Ulwin, if not among the first earls ever created by a Scottish monarch, was at least the first Earl of Lennox of whom history gives any account. He died about 1155 and left a family of young children.

Another Ulwin succeeded to the title and estates towards the close of the 1100's and died in 1225, leaving descendants consisting of Malduin, his heir; Dugald, Rector of the Church of Kilpatrik; Aulay, or MacAulay, whose patrimony was composed of the lands and castle of Faslane and other properties on the Gareloch; Gilchrist who succeeded to the lands of Arrochar and became the founder of Clan Farlane; Christin who, from the number of charters he witnessed, was probably the "Judex de lemmanax", an honour more ancient than the earldom itself; and Cor, whose son Murdoch obtained the lands of Cory.

In 1221 Alexander the 2nd, anxious to encourage trade in the country, granted a charter announcing he had made a Burgh at his new castle at Dumbarton and granted to his Burghers all the liberties enjoyed by the Burgesses of Edinburgh; allowed them a weekly market on Wednesday, and freedom from tolls throughout the county.

In 1224 the same monarch granted the Freemen of Dumbarton and their successors parts of the lands of Morwaich for the common good of the Burgh. Two years later bestowed upon them a third charter granting permission to the Burgesses to hold an annual fair of eight days duration, and conferring them with all the privileges with which such a grant was usually accompanied.

Shortly thereafter there were disputes between the men of Dumbarton and the men of Glasgow regarding the nature and extent of their several privileges. Till the time of William the Lion the villagers of Glasgow were mere men of the Bishop. When they did receive their charter from that monarch between 1175 and 1180, it was not granted them as a body, but to Josalyn, the Bishop, who was to have a Burgh in Glasgow, with a market on Thursdays.

The Freemen of Dumbarton, thinking their charter surpassed this, along with the respective privileges it conferred, endeavoured to prevent the bishop's men from trading either to or past Dumbarton by the Clyde or through the Burgh to the West Highlands, unless the customary tax was paid. For 20 years the burgesses of Dumbarton resisted the claim of the bishop's men to pass tax free through their territory. In 1242 their disputes reached such a height that the peace of the west coast seemed endangered and Alexander the 3rd proposed a fresh charter, granting special exemption to the bishop's men. This arrangement sufficed till the end of the 1400's when it was found necessary, for the preservation of the peace, to draw up a mutual agreement, binding the parties to observe, maintain and defend each others' rights.

In 1238 Malduin, the 3rd Earl, obtained from King Alexander the 2nd a charter confirming him in the Earldom of Lennox as held by Ulwin: excepting the castle of Dumbarton which passed into the hands of the King, and the lands of Morwaich, portions of these having previously been gifted to the Burgh of Dumbarton.

Upon the resignation of the castle of Dumbarton, the chief residence of the Earls of Lennox appears to have been Balloch which, from its contiguity on Loch Lomond and the Leven, must have been a place of considerable importance. Caffer (Drymen) and Faslane were also strongholds occupied either by the Earls themselves or members of their family. Before the close of the 1200's all these places seemed to have been forsaken for a seat on the island of Inchmurrin on Loch Lomond.

Chapter 3   *AD 1250 – 1600*

Vikings – Granting of Clan lands – William Wallace – Robert Bruce – Partition of the Earldom of Lennox

The Burgesses of Dumbarton showed their zest for commerce, but by 1263 Haco, King of Norway, was incensed at what he saw as excesses committed amongst those parts of the western isles he considered his subjects . He decided to lead a force against the King of Scotland to establish for ever the rightful domination of the Norwegian crown over the western isles.

He set off in from Bergen and arrived in the River Clyde in September, 1263. Negotiations broke down, and Haco dispatched Magnus, king of Mann, with a squadron of 60 ships into Loch Long. Included in the party were Prince Dugal, grandson of Reginald, King of the Isles, and Vasel, chief of the Hebrides, together with a large body of his soldiers. They laid waste to the country bordering Loch Long, including the small fort of Danish origin at Knockderry on the Rosneath peninsular. They sailed to the head of Loch Long and went ashore at Arrochar. They learned that the Earl of Lennox and his supporters had taken up residence and refuge in the islands of Loch Lomond. The Norsemen dragged some of their smaller boats across the narrow neck of land between Loch Long and Loch Lomond at Tarbet, which in Gaelic means "passage of the boats".

Many of the Loch Lomond islands housed large numbers of people who were not expecting attack. Most of the peasantry were put to the sword and the country around the loch, then a wealthy and popular district, with villages and fertile lands, was reduced to a smoking desert, strewn with the bodies of its inhabitants and the blackened ruins of its cottages and castles.

From Loch Lomond, Norse chief Allan, brother of Prince Dugal, with a multitude of wild men, penetrated into Dunbartonshire and

Stirlingshire, killing many of the inhabitants, removing whatever items of value they could carry and burning everything else.

The Norsemen returned to Arrochar and secured their plunder in their vessels in Loch Long. Scarcely had they done this than the weather changed. A hurricane blew them from their moorings and reduced ten of the boats to wrecks.

During the three days of the storm, the Scottish soldiery attacked Hako, who was compelled to land the remnants of his force and to engage with Alexander the 3rd's well-equipped army. This encounter ended in the battle of Largs where the Norwegians' hopes of establishing a foothold in Scotland were dashed forever.

Alexander the 2nd made a grant of the Barony of Colquhoun to Umphredus de Kilpatrick, who assumed the name of Colquhoun and joined the lands of Colquhoun with his parish of Kilpatrick, where he built a stronghold on the rock of Dunglas, which still stands adjacent to Bowling, on the riverbank.

In 1225 Maldoven, a near-kinsman of the Earls of Lennox, was given a grant of the lands of Luss by Alwyin, the 2nd earl of Lennox. The family designated themselves De Luss, and the lands continued in the family until they passed by marriage of the heiress of Duncan De Luss to Sir Robert Colquhoun of Colquhoun.

In the later part of the 1200's Malduin, 3rd Earl of Lennox, granted their patrimonies to the Buchanans, the Colquhouns, Galbraiths, McAulays and McFarlanes. In the early part of the 1300's Countess Isabella, daughter of Duncan the 6th Earl of Lennox, married Regent Albany's son Murdoch, thereby uniting the Lennox Earldom with the Earldoms of Monteith and Fife, titles held by Albany. Thus was formed the most powerful and extensive of territorial alliances, overshadowing all other Scottish nobility, even the King.

In 1424 James the 1st was released from 14 years of English imprisonment. Feeling betrayed by the Scottish nobles, James had this Scottish family executed – countess Isabella's father Duncan; her husband, the Duke of Albany, and her two sons were all hanged at

Stirling in 1425. The Lennox Earldom now became partitioned amongst the descendants of Duncan's two daughters, Margaret and Elisabeth. Margaret's daughters married Napier of Merchison and Holdane of Gleneagles and were each awarded one fourth of the Earldom. Elisabeth's grandson, Sir John Stewart of Darnley, was awarded the half earldom, including the title 9th Earl.

Prior to 1238, the principal home of the Earls of Lennox was Dumbarton Castle. It was subsequently resigned to the crown, Mulduin, 3rd Earl of Lennox, receiving in exchange Callander estate near Falkirk. It was around this time that old Balloch Castle, with its stone jetty, was built where the River Leven leaves the loch, thus commanding access to both the Leven and the country up the loch. Opposite the castle in the middle of the Leven was the now-submerged Cairn Island – so called because a cairn had been erected on it to commemorate the tragic drowning of 11 ladies of the Lennox family while bathing from it.

About 1300 the name of William Wallace first appears. His father, Sir Malcolm Wallace of Elderslie, having refused to take the oath of allegiance to the English monarchy, fled with his son to the mountainous districts in the north of the county and took refuge from the vengeance with which they were threatened. Young William soon became celebrated for his independent spirit and brave conduct. An insult received in Lanark from a band of English soldiers and then his slaughter of an English sheriff were amongst the first of a series of events which made him a determined and systematic enemy of the English.

Records of his presence in Dunbartonshire are to be found in his biography written by the minstrel Harry, and also in the unwritten legends. Wallace appears afterwards in the district by being referred to as a conqueror rather than a fugitive. We read that he sacked the town of Dumbarton, laid waste the Castle of Rosneath and then proceeded to Faslane where he was warmly welcomed by his friend and supporter, Malcolm, Earl of Lennox.

In the early 1300's Wallace's luck ran out and a reward of 40 merks was given to the valet who spied out William Wallace, and John of Menteith, second son of the Earl of Menteith, was given a gift of land to the value of one hundred pounds. The capture of Wallace was either in Glasgow or the neighbouring village of Robroyston. Mentieth's duplicity was a key factor. Having convinced Wallace that they were surrounded by soldiers and escape was impossible, he pledged that, if Wallace would allow himself to be carried to Dumbarton, his life would be spared. Wallace submitted and, trusting his old friend Menteith, accompanied him quietly to Dumbarton. He was subsequently taken by force to London where a swift trial and execution followed.

Wallaces' mantle fell to his no-less-worthy successor, Robert Bruce, the grandson of the Bruce who had contested the throne with Baliol. He appears to have taken no very decided steps to set aside the award to the English King, whilst his father, more intent upon lessening the influence of the Baliol and Comyn families than wielding supreme power himself, lent his active assistance to King Edward and appeared in Scotland among the leaders of his army.

The ambition of the younger Bruce was more daring. By turns being the partisan of Edward and of Baliol, he appeared for a time to stifle his own pretensions to the crown, but, as his character developed, this desire gradually became so evident and so deep-rooted as to give firmness and constituency to his whole life.

The capture of Wallace and the murder of Comyn compelled Bruce to adopt open measures of hostility against the English King. Before the remains of the great patriot Wallace had been withdrawn from public gaze, and in the presence of a scanty train, Bruce was crowned King of Scotland at Scone Palace by the Bishop of St Andrews. This act led Bruce to commence a wandering and precarious life among the wilds of his native parish which roused many of the inhabitants to embrace his cause. He was joined by his wife and the wives and sisters of a few of his followers who preferred the perils of life in the woods to the protracted misery that they would undergo if they were captured by the English.

Bruce and his followers retreated further westward to the head of Loch Ewe but this was a part of the country particularly beset with danger. The Comyn faction mustered strong in Argyllshire and every member of the family had vowed vengeance against Bruce for his slaughter of their kinsmen.

Proceeding through a narrow pass near Dalmally, Bruce's party was attacked by a body of Argyll Highlanders. So fierce was the encounter that it was with great difficulty Bruce and two or three more escaped with their lives. It was soon after this defeat that the King resolved to proceed to Ireland. Whilst he was preparing for this journey, he directed his party towards Dunbartonshire where he considered he would not only be safe but welcome, as Malcolm Earl of Lennox had long been the most trusted of his friends.

Bruce appears to have approached Loch Lomond so far southward as to give rise to serious apprehensions of getting across. On reaching the east side of the loch, he searched the shore for a boat in which he and his companions might cross to the lands of the Earl of Malcolm, at Luss – but he was disappointed. After camping overnight in the caves along the shoreline, a small and leaking boat was discovered which at best would hold three people, two of whom would have to bail. It was by this wretched conveyance that Bruce, Douglas and one other landed safely on the west side. Many of the party of two hundred became impatient at the slowness of the process and plunged into the loch fully clothed. They swam across in less time than it took the boat to perform the passage. At this time the level of the loch was much lower and the islands to the immediate south of Luss were joined to the shore.

When the group had gathered on the western bank and rested they divided into two groups and moved to find the Earl of Lennox. He was engaged in the chase in the neighbourhood where Bruce and his party were now hiding. The joy of such a meeting may easily be envisaged, for Lennox rushed into his master's arms and wept aloud. The first emotions of joy having subsided, the Earl observed the haggard state to which his Sovereign and followers were reduced. Without delay he led them to a secure retreat where they sat down to a more hearty meal.

Although the area was the hereditary property of the Lennox family, it was full of friends of the Comyns, who, with other families, controlled the roads and passes. Many of the Earl of Lennox's vassals had been seduced so effectively from their allegiances that they were eager to waylay the King and deliver him to the English leaders. Bruce, therefore, pressed forward to Cantyre, and, in company with Earl Malcolm, they set forth down the Clyde. They avoided some English galleys by a bold and skillful manoeuvre, after which they sailed to the small island of Rachine, about four miles from the north-west part of Ireland.

About 1313 Bruce reappears in Dunbartonshire. Amongst the few fortresses in the west then holding out against him was Dumbarton Castle, commanded by the same Sir John Monteith who had betrayed William Wallace. Menteith had contrived a scheme by which he would obtain a position amongst the nobility of Scotland, secure King Bruce as he had secured Wallace, and at the same time retain possession of the castle.

Menteith professed to surrender himself as a liege of Bruce on condition that he was put in possession of the Earldom of Lennox. Whilst Bruce hesitated in complying with such a demand, Earl Malcolm, one of his staunchest supporters, insisted that Bruce should comply with the governor's request, even though it was not at all reasonable. The magnanimity of the Earl overcame the scruples of Bruce and he agreed to Menteith's demand. A deed setting out the conditions was drawn up and ratified, and all that remained for the King to give it full effect was to take possession of the castle.

On his journey there he came upon a party in the wood of Colquhoun. Roland, a local carpenter, having obtained an audience with the King, informed him that Mentieth had concealed in one of the cellars a strong body of English soldiers who had instructions to come forth when Bruce was seated at dinner and capture him and his attendants.

On touring the castle, Bruce identified a cellar door which was locked and had his attendants break it down. To their dismay they discovered a band of soldiers fully armed, who, interrogated separately, confessed the whole scheme of treachery and said there was a ship of war laying off the castle. It had been commissioned by Menteith to carry Bruce as a prisoner to England.

Whilst Bruce's first impulse was to put Menteith to death, he reflected that he had several powerful relations and therefore deemed advisable to place him under confinement until the eve of the Battle of Bannockburn when he offered Menteith his freedom on condition that he fought with the Scots against the English. Menteith accepted and served faithfully. King Bruce later granted him a full pardon for past deeds.

In the interval between Bannockburn and the final peace of 1328, Bruce strengthened his ties with Dunbartonshire. He built a residence in the parish of Cardross, at that time immediately to the west of the River Leven. It was situated up the road known as Bruce Castle Hill, on a summit overlooking the Vale of Leven and the lower portion of the Vale of Clyde.

A steep ascent on the western side appears to have led to a terrace running along the top of Castlehill on which may have been a single storey building, from 80 to 100 feet in length and about 20 in breadth. Over the years he adorned the interior of his new mansion, extended his pleasure grounds and engaged in the chase. He made experiments in shipbuilding and at other times was found sailing his vessels on the Clyde and harbouring them in the Leven. Bruce is said to have kept a lion and a jester. He entertained the clergy and Barons who visited him at Cardross in truly royal style, although his expenditure was arranged with order and economy. His huntsmen, falconers, dog keepers, gardeners and rangers shared with those of high rank the monarch's abundant hospitality.

In 1328 he contracted a disease which forced him to retire to his palace at Cardross. He died there on the 7th of June 1329 in his 55th year of age, and 24th year of his reign.

In 1443 two of the supporters of Earl Douglas of Lennox had an altercation over the possession of Dumbarton Castle and one of them was killed. Douglas was anxious about the effect of such violence on his supporters, and, with well-feigned humility, sought an interview with the young King James the 2nd. He gave the Earl a full remission and afterwards admitted him into his most secret of councils. In 1445 the Castle of Dumbarton, along with the lands of Cardross, Rosneath, the annual rent of Tadyow and the payment of dues known as the "Watch Meal of Kilpatrick", were formally annexed to the Crown.

Earl Douglas's eldest daughter, the Countess Isobella, died about 1460. As the Countess had not exercised the rights of a feudal superior during her lifetime, and it was unclear if she had obtained formal entry into the estates held by her father, the King took advantage and assigned the revenue of the Earldom of Lennox for the building of the castle in Stirling.

It is sometime said that Robert the Bruce might lay claim to being the father of the emerging Scottish navy. During his last days he built craft and enjoyed sailing. His leadership and enthusiasm possibly caused James the 4th in 1511, after much anxiety and cost, to launch his ambitious warship The Mittle. She was 240 feet long, and was said to be the wonder of the seas, for her hull was made of oak 10 feet thick. Arguably this marked the beginning of shipbuilding in Dumbarton.

In the year 1511 the Earls of Lennox still had a castle at Balloch, whose name in the old Scots means "field of the pass". The wooden castle was constructed on the shore of the loch near where the modern Balloch Castle is situated. It had a foss, or moat, which could be flooded, and a drawbridge. However, the castle on Inchmurrin remained the chief dwelling of the Earls of Lennox.

After the partition of the Earldom ,which was disputed by Duncan's illegitimate child, the family of Lennox of Woodhead believed the Earldom should be theirs. As the son of the 12th Earl Henry, Lord Darnley married Mary Queen of Scots in 1565. Balloch was subsequently claimed by the Darnleys who frequently entertained royalty and laid out a tennis court. Inchmurrin became a hunting lodge patronised by royalty The area around Balloch continued in the hands of the Darnley branch of the house of Lennox until 1652, when James, the 4th Duke of Lennox, sold Balloch to Sir John Colquhoun of Luss, along with his fishings in Loch Lomond and the Leven.

For the purpose of this book it is sufficient to note that the Earldom of Lennox passed down through succeeding generations and was interwound with the various monarchs and custodians of Dumbarton Castle and the surrounding lands. The history of this period would fill a lengthy book in its own right and it is no part of this story to go into those details which are dealt with excellently by others. Suffice to say that the Earl of Lennox was made Regent to the infant King in 1570, and his favours continued, because in August 1581 King James created the Earldom of Lennox into a dukedom to advance his favourite Esmee, and elevated him also to the office of Lord High Chamberlain of Scotland. With the exceptional case of Queen Mary's third husband Bothwell created Duke of Orkney, this was the first time the dignity of a dukedom had been confirmed on anyone not directly a member of the royal family.

The duke moved for a period to France where he died in May, 1583, his illness arising principally from excessive grief.

For a period the governorship of Dumbarton Castle was conferred upon Lord John, the second son of James, Earl of Arran, who held it until 1594. In 1598 it passed into the hands of Lennox's son Ludevic, whom James had brought to Scotland and raised to all the honours which had been conferred on his early favourite Duke Esmee.

From the close of the 16th Century till the time of the great civil war few events of interest occurred in connection with the castle of Dumbarton. The peace which ensued upon the union of the crowns greatly lessened the importance of the fortress site at Dumbarton. This is considered an era in which many of our national strongholds were either transformed into simple residences or deserted.

So long as James remained in Scotland – and even after he ascended the English throne – he manifested in many ways his attachments to the Lennox. In the Charge of Confirmation, which he granted in 1609 to the Burgh of Dumbarton, special mention is made of the attendance of the Burgesses on "our Royal Persons in all journeying's and hunting's in these parts, especially in the Island of Inchmurrin". Their hospitality to the nobility and domestics who tended him on such occasions, as well as the protection they afforded, ensured a peaceable environment.

Chapter 4   AD 1600 – 1775

Formation of Parishes – Development of Roads and Bridges – Textiles in the Vale of Leven – The Development of Canals.

The Gareloch was a glacial valley in the Ice Age and Rhu Peninsula is formed from terminal moraine, left behind by the glacier as it melted.

Handed down from the days of Gaelic, we find that the original name of what is now Rhu was "Rhue", or point of land. Parishes were often named from the locality selected for the Kirk and this appears to have been the case with Rhu. The name of the locality was commonly Rhue of Conel, applicable to the remarkable promontory in the Gareloch which in earlier times approached much nearer to Rosneath than now. In the early 1600's there were two parishes adjoining Rhu, Rosneath and Cardross, the boundary between Rhu and the latter probably lying towards the eastern end of the modern Helensburgh.

In those days it appears from ecclesiastical records that a place of subordinate worship for the accommodation of the local population was an "Ease". By an act of general assembly in August 1639 the Rosneath presbytery was empowered to take measures for settling both parishes of Rosneath and Cardross with an "ease" in between.

When the presbytery began their proceedings in February 1640 "the Kirk upon the Rhue of Conel" was proposed and McAulay of Ardencaple required the "ease" to be there. At another meeting, held the same month, Mr George Lindsay, minister of Rosneath, offered security to maintain a helper, but Mr Robert Walton, minister of Cardross, rather than any part of his parish be united to Rosneath, made a large offer for building a church and maintaining a helper in Glen Fruin.

There ensued a long and keen conflict between contending parties. The minister of Rosneath ,instead of being disburdened of the part of his charge east of Gareloch, was charged with having to preach every second Sabbath at the Kirk of Rhu. In 1643 the Lords Commissioners for the Plantation of Kirks decreed the disjunction. As much of Rosneath lying to the east of Kirkmichael (in current days the east boundary of Helensburgh) was annexed to Cardross as was disjoined from Cardross to be annexed to the Kirk of Row. The part of Cardross taken to make up the new parish embraced the Bannachra, Glen Fruin and the lands about Garelochhead. The compensation received by Cardross from Rosneath lay between Kirkmichael and the Cardross church. At that time the church stood on Cardross point at the confluence of the Leven with the Clyde.

The road between Helensburgh and Rhu in those days was narrow and indifferently preserved, leading along the margin of the Gareloch. Immediately on leaving Helensburgh, Ardencaple Castle and its policies appeared at the side of the road, the castle being of some antiquity and local historical interest. It stood on a rising knoll, defended by an array of stately trees by whose leafy branches it was almost wholly concealed in the summer. The early 1600's were confusing times. The part of Rhu parish which extended from Shandon to the east boundary of Helensburgh belonged to Rosneath, but from Shandon to Garelochhead and the Strath of Glen Fruin belonged to Cardross. From Garelochhead to the boundary of the parish of Arrochar is mentioned in the report of the commissioners in 1630 as lying in the parish of Inshalloch, an old parish which is now unknown and seems to have merged into the parish of Cardross.

The district now comprising the parish of Rhu, although not a parish until 1646, possessed several places of worship, one at Faslane, where the Lennox family had a castle, and where a considerable part of the chapel still stands in the Faslane Cemetery. Another was in Glen Fruin, to which considerable church lands were attached. The only remnant is the stone baptismal font built into the wall of the schoolmaster's house. There was another church at Kirkmichael in Helensburgh of which no vestige remains, though religious services were said to be performed there in the early part of the 1700's by an indulgent Episcopal minister.

When the Rhu parish was formed the most populous portion of it was the now almost deserted Glen of the Fruin where it was first intended that parish church should be placed. The tenantry, however, succeeded in getting it erected where it now stands by giving land for the church, church yard and glebe. The first minister was chosen for his ability to preach Gaelic, but, although that tongue has long since ceased to be used in preaching or conversation, it is still recorded in the late 1800's.

After the end of the 1689 revolution against James the 2nd and the settling of the crown on the Prince and Princess of Orange, benefits began to be felt in the southern part of the Dumbarton county. Trade developed and expanded rapidly. In the northern parts of the county remnants of the turbulent clans, who saw opportunities for pilfering in the confusion following the disputed succession, revived their old ways and excesses. In 1690 an Act of Parliament restored the old enactments against the MacGregors.

This Act also made the hereditors of Dunbartonshire and Stirlingshire liable for all depredations committed within their boundaries. The industrious people in the southern part of the county appeared willing to purchase security through blackmail with the unruly clans, and payments were made to leave land alone. The unruly, blackmailing clans used approximately one half of their funds and resources to recover stolen cattle and the other half to steal them in order to make blackmail necessary. This ingenious method of living continued for a number of years.

After the repression of the Jacobite rebellion in 1745, the government saw value in having a reasonable road network and Acts of Parliament were passed which created the turnpike roads and highways, and designated the districts into which they were to be organised. The roads were to be constructed and maintained in the early years by soldiers funded by forfeited Jacobite estates. During the second half of the 1700's our area, designated the western district, was formed into many individual trusts for the management of individual roads.

In the Western District, the third Kilmarnock trust covered the construction of the road from Drymen Bridge to Dumbarton, a total of 15 miles, on which there were three tolls. The Fourth or Helensburgh trust covered the road from Dumbarton to the north boundary of Helensburgh at Ardencaple Gate, a road of eight miles, embracing two tolls. The fifth, or Luss trust, covered the road from Dumbarton, via Tarbet, to Loch Long Head (in modern terminology Arrochar), with branches en route to Helensburgh from Redhouse and Douchlage, a total of 40 miles incorporating eight tolls. The sixth Gareloch and Loch Long trust covered the road built from the north boundary of Helensburgh along the shores of the Gareloch and Loch Long to the bridge at Loch Long Head (now Arrochar), a total of 17 miles with three tolls.

The Colquhouns gradually acquired most parts of the highland parishes within Dunbartonshire. They set-up a country house at Rossdhu and enclosed much land after 1775. The Duke of Argyll retained the part of Rosneath parish which his family had received as a gift from the crown in 1489 and there built Rosneath Castle, one of his country houses.

The importance of Dumbarton as a military centre declined and the town, which had lost its chance of becoming Glasgow's out port, was of little importance until 1800's when the ship builders put it on the map. An Act of Parliament in 1770 encouraged improvements in the entailed estates and many enclosures took place, drainage was improved and new methods of farming were adopted. By the end of the 1700's about two thirds of the land was enclosed and industry had started.

Farming in the 1700's consisted of many small crofts providing accommodation and subsistence for individual families. Many areas were very populous. One example is Glen Fruin, where many small

35

farms have been amalgamated over the centuries into the few large ones remaining. Evidence of the crofts has long since passed. Some of these small crofts were located in places where the modern reader would find the environment totally inhospitable and unmanageable.

Main roads in the county were supposed to be maintained, according to an Act of 1719, by compulsory labour of so many days work per year from every able-bodied man, but little real work was done on such "parish roads days". In the second half of the 1700's various Acts were passed to enable landowners to set up turnpikes on the road at which tolls were charged – the money to be used for maintaining the road. A tollhouse was built at the turnpike with a tollbar and all traffic had to halt till payment was made. There were many of these tolls and some of the names are still used, although the tollhouses have nearly all disappeared since the abolition of charges in 1883. One does remain – the Tollhouse on the left hand side at the top of Sinclair Street has recently been renovated.

Bridges were also built and improved. Those at Bonhill and Balloch were toll bridges for the benefit of the local landowners, Smollett and Colquhoun, who had funded the building. Dumbarton Bridge, for which stones had been collected for almost a hundred years, was completed in 1765. Before that time, traffic crossed by ferry, but it was largely due to the influence of the Duke of Argyll, who frequently went through Dumbarton on his way to Inverary or Rosneath castle, that the bridge was built.

The pure, clear water along the Leven began in the 1700's to attract textile work to the surrounding areas. The water was suitable for bleaching linen and large bleach fields extending to 12 acres, were laid out in 1727 at Dalquhurn. Workmen were brought over from Holland to introduce Dutch methods. These involved laying out the unbleached linen on hedges between which water was brought in narrow channels so that the linen could be soaked at regular intervals and dried again in the sun, the process taking several weeks during the summer. Another bleach field was laid out a little way up the river from Dalquhurn on the loop at Cordale. It was because of the number of employees at these two bleachfields, that in 1762 Mrs Smollett of Bonhill founded a village which she named after her daughter-in-law whose maiden name was Cecilia Renton.

The first print work in the Vale of Leven was started in 1768, further up the river at Levenfield printfields, where they worked on cotton instead of linen. The population almost trebled. Nearly a thousand were employed in the printfields, while the seasonal occupation of bleaching attracted highlanders in the summer months, some of them, in time, settling as residents. It was not until the 1800's that the village opposite Bonhill church – known as "Grocery" because it had a shop of that kind – received the name of Alexandria, after the proprietor of the land, Alexander Smollett.

Before the days of railways, heavy traffic had to go by water, and it was to carry coal from the Monkland area to Glasgow that James Watt surveyed the Monkland Canal in 1769. It was not opened until 1792. He was also employed on the surveys for the Forth and Clyde canal and favoured a canal up the Vale of Leven to Loch Lomond and from there across to the Forth. The Glasgow merchants, who provided most of the money for building the canal, naturally did not favour this project which would by-pass the city. When the canal was begun in 1768, under the supervision of James Smeaton, the famous builder of Edison Lighthouse, it was planned to run from near Grangemouth to Glasgow, and then, as the Clyde was so shallow in those days, by a parallel line with the Clyde down to deep water at Bowling.

Because of financial difficulties during the American War of Independence and for some years thereafter, its terminus was on the outskirts of Glasgow, but it was completed in 1790 with a branch from Maryhill to the Monkland canal and another branch to join the Clyde opposite the Cart, giving access to Paisley. The Forth and Clyde canal, terminating now at Bowling, was opened officially in 1790 and a hogshead of water was brought from the Forth and poured into the Clyde, symbolising the union of the seas. It is said that the use of the wheelbarrow in the district dates from the construction of the canal.

The shallowness of the Clyde was for long a great hindrance to the Glasgow merchants, and there were seven places between Glasgow Green and Dumbarton where the river could be forded at low tide. It was because of this shallowness that Glasgow merchants built a harbour at Port Glasgow in 1668. They first approached the Dumbarton people with a proposal to build a harbour there, but the Dumbarton Town Council declined, partly because of the long-standing dispute with Glasgow over rights in the Clyde. By the end of the 1700's Glasgow had also carried out a deepening of the Clyde that allowed the larger ships access. Before the river was deepened it spread itself at high tide over a large area, and Dumbarton rock became an island; but the deepening of the channel and the building of jetties along the banks made it possible to reclaim much low-lying land (hence Whiteinch in Glasgow, and Abbotsinch in Renfrew – 'inch' standing for an island).

Chapter 5   *AD 1603*

Conflict in Glen Fruin

The battle between the Colquhouns and the McGregors in Glen Fruin is a known fact, but no authoritative account of the reasons for the conflict have been handed down

There are numerous accounts of bad blood between them from the latter part of the 16th century. The lands of Clan McFarlane at the head of Loch Lomond were little more than rugged mountains, and those of the McGregors on the eastern shore largely resembled them. On the other hand the lands of Luss afforded fair pasture for cattle and yielded crops of corn. It was part of the simple philosophy of the highland mind to equalise the distribution of goods

The McFarlanes and McGregors in concert were in the habit of relieving the Colquhouns of their assets on moonlit nights. In about 1590 the clans again made a determined foray onto the lands of Luss, and, either in pursuit of spoil or revenge, were met by Sir Humphrey Colquhoun, the 14th of the line, and engaged in battle. The Colquhouns were defeated, and Sir Humphrey was obliged to beat a retreat to the castle of Bannachra at the foot of Ben Buie hill. This castle, as maybe judged from its remains, was not only a strong building but occupied rising ground and an admirable position for defence. It might have been successfully held had not Sir Humphrey shown himself at a loophole where an archer saw him and slew him. Tradition has it that a traitor in his service lit by a torch his position to the enemy and thus secured his death.

At that time Archibald, Duke of Argyll, was the King's lieutenant in this area. Such commission put into the hands of crafty and designing statesmen like Archibald powers which they could use for their own benefit, and it is believed that the Argylls stirred up discontent amongst other clans as a means of getting their own back against their own personal foes. On good authority it is believed that this was the way by which the McGregors were incited into acts of hostility against the Colquhouns.

It was a bleak February morning in 1603, the hills clad with snow and a biting frosty wind, when the war broke out. A mile or so along Glen Fruin, coming from the west and just past the farm of Strone, there is a glen down which the Auchengaith burn comes into view. It was through this glen the McGregors descended to Glen Fruin the night before the battle.

Allister McGregor, chief of the clan, and his brother John were accompanied by about 300 men. It is probable that the number of the Colquhouns was equal to this, but certainly considerably fewer than the 800 which has been suggested. The McGregors' superior military tactics were manifest. They divided into two bodies, one of which, led by Allistair, occupied the upper part of the glen, while the men under the control of his brother lay concealed near its foot. The battle met somewhere in the vicinity of Strone farm, where at times the struggle was keen and fierce. The McGregors, long accustomed to guerrilla warfare in these highland recesses, triumphed and the Colquhouns were driven back into the ambush laid by John McGregor (who seems to have been slain in the conflict). They were pursued to Rossdhu, a distance of about six miles, where a fearful scene of bloodshed and plunder ensued.

The farm buildings and shielings in and near the glen were entered and their inmates cruelly butchered; the houses burned, and the cattle carried off. In the indictment laid against chief Allister, the cattle were described as 600, together with 800 sheep and goats and 14 score of horses.

About 140 Colquhouns were killed in the battle or retreat, while the loss of McGregors seems not to have exceeded more than a few men. Tradition has it that the victorious McGregors, inflamed with victory, wantonly murdered some 30 or 40 boys, students in the Collegiate institution in Dumbarton, who had been spectators of the fight. They had been gathered in a house near Bannachra and placed under a guard for protection, but at the close of the day, when the chief of the McGregors enquired after them, he found that certain of his followers, in the absence of the guard, had butchered them all.

The McGregors returned to their native fastness with their booty where they were welcomed by the clan; but the arm of the law caught up with them when Sir Alexandra Colquhoun appeared before King James the 6th at Stirling. This was followed by an Act of Privy Council advising extermination of the clan and making it an offence punishable by death to give any of them food or shelter. They were consequently pursued and hunted, their leaders executed, their possessions destroyed and their children either put to death or committed to the tender mercies of some lawless chief and forbidden to bear the name of McGregor.

If the Duke of Argyll had been behind the conflict, his ambitions were thwarted when the Colquhouns retained their lands and gradually rebuilt the clan, in due course founding the town of Helensburgh.

Chapter 6   AD 1776 – 1799

Millig – Advertisement of Fue's – Earliest Helensburgh Developments – Development of Industry.

Sir James Colqhoun, the 15th baronet, lived during the middle part of the 1700's and died in 1786. He married Lady Helen Sutherland, celebrated for her talents, personal attractions and useful life, and whose name was eventually adopted as the title of Helensburgh.

It was Sir James who in 1756 purchased the lands which eventually became Helensburgh from Sir John Shaw Stuart of Greenock for the sum of six thousand five hundred pounds. He was obviously of an acquisitive nature as he also purchased Faslane for one thousand two hundred and fifty pounds, Ardenconnel for five thousand pounds and the Clyde and Leven fishings for two and a half thousand pounds. It was he who commenced the building of the present Rossdhu House to which he moved in 1774.

At that time the shoreline of the area on which Helensburgh now stands was very different. There were distinctive east and west bays which came much further inland, and to the west of the east bay was a substantial promontory of land. It has subsequently been washed away. To the west of the west bay a substantial area of land was also swallowed by the sea. There was no sea wall or demarcation and the sandy beach ran up into what is now Clyde Street and beyond. There was no building along the beach front, except for nine small thatched fishermen's cottages, long since gone. The only other buildings were the ferryman's cottage at Drumfork from which a ferry to Greenock operated, this being the terminus of the Old Luss road. There was also Ardencaple Castle and its estate, inland from what eventually became Kidston Park, in which there was an inn and two fishermen's cottages. The area was known as Cairndhu Point and the Cairndhu Inn was situated here, the home of the Duke of Argyll's boatman (the area was known after him as Neddy's point). There was no road or track along the seashore, but the main thoroughfare from Dumbarton passed by the Drumfork ferry and then onwards to Rhu, passing on the seaward side of Ardencaple Castle.

The area was known as Millig, after the corn mill which had operated from the early 1700's in the location eventually to become Hermitage Park. The Millig burn ran into a mill lade in part of the park now covered by the bowling green and tennis courts. From there the water could be controlled over a water wheel in the Millig mill, the remnants of which can still be seen on the banks of the burn, behind the Victoria Halls.

There was an old chapel in the east end of the town known as Kirkmichael, although its precise whereabouts can no longer be traced. Upstream from the corn mill lies an area known as Chapelacre, through which the Millig Burn flows. It was recorded in 1830 that the ruins of a chapel, also called Kirkmichael, and a hermitage could still be traced.

The hillside embraced the lands on which seven farms were situated, starting from the east with Stuckenduff; the upper part of the town East Millig and mid Millig; and to the western end Woodend Farm. Although the names are not known, the single storey building in East King Street, opposite the present medical centre, was a farm house, and at the other end of the town a single storey building, directly behind the now Commodore Hotel, was a farm. Similarly at the extreme west end of Princes Street there is another farm house, currently occupied as a residence. The woods and policies surrounding Ardencaple Castle came right down to the foreshore on which there was a profusion of sloes and light vegetation. The waterfront was covered with golden sands which subsequently became an attraction for visitors

The exact circumstances and timing of the sea reclaiming the two foreshores in the east and west bays and removing the sand are not recorded, but in the year 1767 and into the early 1800's there was land on the foreshore – and up to 1939 golden sands. It can be speculated that the building of the pier and dredging of the river may have redirected the currents along the foreshore

In the early 1760's Scotland was recovering from a financial and cash crisis and many estate owners were obliged to sell their estates at reduced values. It seems safe to assume that Sir James Colquhoun was not immune to these pressures and that his way of alleviating financial hardship was to offer the land to be feued which would potentially bring in many times the rent obtainable from letting of farms. He was probably influenced by seeing how effectively the towns of Greenock and Gourock were evolving across the water by encouraging manufacturing and trading.

The first public notice concerning the area appears in the *Glasgow Journal* newspaper on 11th January 1776, 20 years after Sir James had purchased the land, and is in the following terms

> NOTICE — to be feued immediately, for building upon at a very reasonable rate, a considerable piece of ground upon the shores of Mallig, opposite Greenock. The land lies on both sides of the road leading from Dumbarton to the Kirk of Row. The ground will be regularly laid out for houses and gardens to be built according to a plan. There is a freestone quarry on the ground.
> For the accommodation of the feuars the proprietor is to enclose a large field for grazing their milk cows
> N.B. bonnets makers, stocking, linen and woollen weavers will meet with proper encouragement. There is a large boat building at the place for ferrying men and horses with chaises.

At this date the town was nameless and continued to be referred to as the new town for some years to come.

As late as the late 1700's the few strangers who ventured into the backwater of the Gareloch discovered that the natives had no interest

44

in the outer world. Whistlefield Inn demonstrates the desire of travellers to pass rapidly through the area and indicates the wishes of the rider not to dismount, whistling for the attention of mine host to fetch a stirrup cup of ale. Before the age of steam, ferrymen transported passengers and livestock. They knew what was transpiring from wayfarers and their gossip was eagerly devoured by lovers of local news and scandal.

In the late 1700's necessity at last caused the carriageway to take shape along the northern shore of the Gareloch. It was rough and narrow, and followed its sinuous course around each inlet and over each hillock. It afforded a wonderful vista up and down the loch, and numerous national figures passed this way, including Mary Queen of Scots, who enjoyed many happy days hereabout, enjoying the royal sport of falconry, with her loyal friend Sir John, the 13th Master of Colquhoun, and Robert Burns. Other worthies included the itinerant taylors, tinkers, cobblers and packmen.

The miseries of poverty were mitigated by a universal cheerfulness, unperturbed by the urge for better housing, hot and cold water, or the need for sanitary conveniences. Food and drink were good and cheap and everyone did as they pleased. The Laird was regarded as a demi-god with his genial sociableness, and his community was a family.

Up till about 1800 there was negligible progress and indeed in 1802 it is recorded that there were only 17 premises within what became the Burgh of Barony of Helensburgh. As to bonnet makers and the rest, the "proper encouragement" was not forthcoming. They simply never materialised, and the large ferry boat was probably never finished.

About the year 1800 a few houses, not exceeding a dozen, were standing on the line of the turnpike road leading to Row and Arrochar. They were of unpretentious design, some roofed with thatch, others with tiles. The most imposing stood at the west of the foot of Sinclair Street, adorned with a bow window and slated roof. It was still there in 1900 but we can only guess what befell it.

Travellers passing through Helensburgh in the 1790's on the way to

Loch Lomond referred to it as a small village, even then acquiring a reputation for sea bathing. This is certainly the earliest activity associated with Helensburgh and no doubt played a large part in attracting many of the earliest inhabitants. Only two buildings in the neighbourhood are mentioned by name, Ardenconnel House, "an elegant modern building" owned by Andrew Buchanan, and Ardencaple Castle. About this time, the Glasgow merchants, or more probably their wives, found that it was beneficial for the health of their families to quit the tempting gaieties of Glasgow during a summer month and spend it on the coast. Helensburgh and Gourock were then the only easily available resorts. They were reached by posting or carrier's wagon, the wagon being preferred because of its more ample accomodatiom for bairns and furnishings. It was also a leisurely mode of travelling, satisfying our sedate forefathers.

There was still another mode of transport – by flyboat which left the Broomielaw daily, tide permitting. The flyboat, despite its title, often grounded on sand banks and remained fast until the return of the flood tide. A change of wind or adverse tide often stalled its progress, during which time the highland boatmen generally went ashore to refresh at a convenient public house, leaving the passengers to view the scenery.

It seems incongruous that, apart from inns, the first public building in Helensburgh was a theatre built at the very end of the 1700's on the corner of Sinclair Street and Princes Street, where future town halls and municipal offices were to be found. The theatre had been supported mainly by the surrounding county gentlemen, although it had limited success and a brief existence. From 1809 the building started to be used as a magistrates' court, there being no other public buildings in the town. By the 1820's the building housed a library, established by public subscription of £4 a share, owned by householders connected with the town. This was located within the walls of the old town theatre with the pit and boxes forming the court hall. Inside the theatre building, where actors were once wont to 'strut and fret their art upon the stage', there was a grocery store and police cells. The gallery was devoted to rats and spare lumber. The subscription library proprietors continued until 1850, when the institution was disbanded and the books divided by lot amongst the shareholders.

Councillors' attempts to construct a town house made for a curious episode. In November 1807, the Provost and Senior Bailie purchased ground opposite the house of Daniel Colquhoun, on behalf of the "City of Helensburgh" for a town house, and this was approved. In April 1808 council accepted the offer of John Bramender to build it for two hundred and sixty pounds or two hundred and forty five pounds "if twenty feet were kept off the steeple". Yet a few weeks later the plan was scrapped, the ground given up and eighty pounds paid to Sir James Colquhoun to compensate him for not taking up the feu.

Throughout the 1700's there was a great trade in Highland cattle and Crieff Fair and later Falkirk Tryst were the largest cattle fairs in Scotland. The latter was a mecca for Highland drovers and cattle dealers from the Lowlands and England. Cattle from Argyll passed through Dunbartonshire, the drovers crossing the Leven by Dumbarton bridge or by the fords at Bonhill and thereafter driving their cattle across Dumbarton muir.

In addition to the major fairs and weekly markets in the large towns of Dumbarton and Kirkintilloch, there were two fairs of some importance that attracted drovers and dealers from a distance. These were the Dumbarton Horse and Cattle Fair on Carman Hill, above the modern Cardross and Renton, which was held in August, and the Moss'o'Balloch Horse Fair in September. Above Carman reservoir today can still be seen the site where hundreds of horses and cattle were bought and sold. The drove roads leading to it from north, east, south and west.

Whilst the fair was on Renton was a busy place, and sometimes evenings brought brawling and disorder in clashes between the drovers, the cotton printers from the Vale of Leven or the shipwrights from Dumbarton.

Coal mining in Dunbartonshire developed in small pockets at various times from the late 1600's onwards. The nearest coalfield was at Duntocher and this was exploited to a small extent by William Dunn. Coal was mined in an increasingly from about 1820. After 1840 most of the early mines were near Kirkintilloch. In the middle of the 1800's mining villages like Croy and Twechar began to grow. In New Kilpartick, mining was extended from the 1860's. At its peak the output of coal in 1900 was a little over 500,000 tons. There were just over 2,000 coal miners, but the industry died away in the early part of the 1900's.

The mining of iron ore in coal-producing areas was extremely important from the transportation point of view, especially in the period from 1760 to 1860 when the railway building era called for substantial iron production. The Kirkintilloch district was one of the main regions for mining iron ore and coal. The Carron Ironworks at Falkirk were one of the first and largest ironworks and used coke instead of charcoal for smelting from 1760. One of the first furnaces built after the Carron Ironworks was that of the Dalnotter Iron Company which started up in Dalmuir in 1769. It moved up to Duntocher in 1776 to make use of water power. Some of the iron it supplied was used in a spade forge and a nail factory nearby.

The main industry in Dumbarton in the 1700's was glass making. At the glass works were three large cones, or kilns, the largest in Scotland. They were set up in 1777 by the Dixon family and were run by them until 1830 when three of the partners – the father and two sons – died within a very short time. There was local consternation when it closed in 1831, having dominated the economic and social life of the town. It re-opened again in 1838 but finally closed in 1850, following the removal of import duty on foreign glass in 1846.

The Dixons at one time paid almost £120,000 per annum in excise duty on their glass manufacture, and they were amongst one of the wealthiest in Scotland. They depended for some of their raw material on kelp (burnt seaweed from the western isles), and their mansion house, Levengrove, was used extensively for luxurious entertaining. Amongst its visitors was Robert Burns, on his trip to Dumbarton in 1787. In the modern day Levengrove Park is now one of the finest in the country.

The soft and mud-free water of the Leven were ideal for bleaching and printing and in these areas grew the first industrial concentration in the county, where small factories with power-driven machinery for spinning and weaving of textiles were built along little fast-flowing streams. Milton, by Bowling, claims to have had the first power loom in Scotland.

Chapter 7   AD 1791 The Statistical Account.

Rhu – New Port-Glasgow – Gourock – Greenock – Luss – Cardross –
Rosneath.

In 1770 the government in London decreed that a statistical account of Scotland would be prepared. This was probably an act of stocktaking following the union of the crowns earlier in the century.

It was decreed that the minister of each of the 843 parishes in Scotland should write his account of the status and economy of his parish. As would be expected, the styles, detail and content varied substantially from parish to parish. At that time the only parishes in our immediate area were those of Rhu, Arrochar, Luss, Rosneath Cardross, Greenock, Gourock and New Port-Glasgow.

* * *

The minister at Row (Rhu) was the Reverend John Allen and an abbreviated version of his discourse follows;

The name Row is a Gaelic word which signifies point. Very near the place where the church is situated there is a pretty long point running out into the sea. The parish is situated in the presbytery of Dumbarton and the sinod of Glasgow and Ayr. It is between 13 and 14 miles in length and about 3 in breadth bounded on the east by the parish of Cardross the north east by Luss and the north west by Loch Long, and the west and south by the Gareloch which separates it from Rosneath and the Firth of Clyde which separates it from Greenock.

The east end of the parish is pretty flat although the greatest part of it is hilly and towards the northeast mountainous. The soil in general is light and where it is properly cultivated pretty fertile. The air is sharp and healthy. Fevers are the prevalent distempers. The sea coast extends for 12 miles, for most part flat and sandy with in some places higher and rocky. Salmon, haddocks, small cod, whiting, small flounders and sometimes mackerel and herring are caught in the lochs before mentioned. The quantities are not great. Salmon is sold at 6d the lb., mackerel ¹/₂ d the piece haddocks etc 1¹/₂ d a lb. The best season for salmon is from the beginning of April to the end of July: mackerel in June and July: Haddocks from December to March: cod and whiting in the summer months. Salmon herring and mackerel are taken with nets the other species with long or hand lines.

The town of Greenock is the principal market. Species of Whales called bottle-noases, have sometimes run aground during the tide of ebb been taken and oil extracted from them. Porpoises and seals are likewise to be seen. Seaware is often used along the coast for manuring land, and kelp is sometimes made but in very small quantities. 20 or 30 years ago all the hills were covered with heaths but since the introduction and increase of sheep the heath has gradually lessened and the hills have began to have a greener appearance.

Population – about 50 or 60 years ago it appears the amount of the population was about 1,300. The present amount is about 1,000 the number males 486 females 514. It appears from the register that there are more males born than females but many of the young men leave the parish in quest of employment some as sailors others as tradesmen or servants. There is one village in the parish lately built which contains about a 100 soles *[the author assumes this is a reference to the new town or Helensburgh as it became known]*. The annual average of births is approximately 40. There is no distinct register of burials prior to 1783 nor can the number of deaths be exactly ascertained now that it is kept because some of the people have their burying places in neighbouring parishes and some from other parishes brought here. The annual average however may be about 14. The annual average of marriages is approx. 9 per year

There are in the parish 65 farmers, their families are about 325 in number. The population has already been observed has decreased the last 10 or 20 years owing to many of the farms now being populated by 1 tenant which were formerly occupied by 3 or 4 and sometimes more, each of whom accommodated a cottager. Besides some of the farms have late years been entirely kept under grass and no tenant on the grounds. Each marriage at an average produces about 6 children.

Agriculture – there are from 4,500 to 5,000 sheep and the average price of white wool 7 shillings the stone and the wool laid with tar 5 shillings. The parish does more than supply itself with provisions, Greenock is the market of over plus for grain and potatoes, Glasgow, Paisley, Port Glasgow, Greenock and Dumbarton for beef, mutton etc. Oats and peas are sown from the 20th March, potatoes from the middle of April. The crops are reaped in general from the beginning of September to the 20th October.

The value of the living, including the glebe is about 100 guineas and the Duke of Argyll is the patron. The church was re-built in the year 1763 and the manse in 1737. There are 8 heritors: 1 small proprietor that resides constantly and another occasionally.

There are 2 schools : the salary of the parochial school master amounts to 80 Scots pounds per year. During the winter there are generally from 30 to 40 scholars and in summer about half that number : his emoluments including a session clerk dues scarce amount to 13 pounds sterling a year – about 30 years ago one of the then heritors of the parish Mr Glen of Portincaple mortified a piece of land for the support of another school master : the number of scholars taught by him is considerably greater and his emoluments are least equal to the parochial one. There are present 8 poor who receive regular supply and about the same number occasionally. The farms have a weekly collection at the church door amounting to from 10 pounds to 12 pounds a year together with the interest on about 220 pounds of stock , 50 pounds of which was lately bequeathed by Robert Carmichael of Broomly a late proprietor of Bonhill.

Prices, wages – the present price of beef veal and mutton 6d a lb., butter from 9d to 10d a lb., cheese from 4s to 6s a stone, a hen from 1s to 1s 3d. These articles of provisions have doubled in price from what they were 40 years ago.

The wages for labourers in husbandry are from 10d to 1s a day. The usual wages of menservants employed in husbandry are from 8 to 9 pounds a year, females from 3 to 4 pounds. The fuel commonly made use of by the tenants is peat or turf which is cut on the moors of the respective farms. Coals are likewise brought from the neighbourhood of Glasgow the price of which is greatly increased of late years.

Miscellaneous observations – there are several remains of popeish chapels, within the last 20 or 30 years have been found in different places one of which was 4 stones set upon edge with a large flag covering them. The opening about $4^{1}/_{2}$ feet by $2^{1}/_{2}$. in which human bones were deposited.

The people are fond of the sea faring life during the last war from 25 to 30 able bodied seamen from this parish were employed in the navy but they are not fond of a military one. The people in general are not expensive. A few individuals are much addicted to dram drinking and the young people especially the females fond of dress more expensive and outwith that which their circumstances can afford.

There are about 11 ale or rather whiskey hoofs, one properly being called an Inn, being one of the stages on the line of road lately made by the Duke of Argyll between Inverary and Dumbarton – English is generally spoken but many understand and frequently converse in Gaelic.

* * *

The Reverend John Forrest wrote 19 pages in his statistical account of the parish of New Port-Glasgow and records that:

It was a modern parish the ancient name of which, being only a small village, was Newark. It was formerly a part of the parish of Kilmalcolm but the magistrates and council of Glasgow having, in the year 1668, feued about 11 acres of land adjoining the old village upon which they erected a harbour for the accommodation of their shipping.

The council of Glasgow foreseeing that it was likely soon to become a populous place applied with the concurrence of all concerned to the Lords of the Plantation of Kirks and got it enacted into a separate parish in the year 1695.

The parish is nearly an English mile square and the land is partly flat, partly mountainous. Along the coast and for 130 yards inland is nearly dead level a little higher than the water mark and this flat part except for that part on which the town stands is presently entirely converted into garden ground belonging to the inhabitants who grow with astonishing effect all kinds of herbs, common fruits both small and big and of the richest quality and in the greatest abundance.

The air of the parish is moist owing it is supposed to its vicinity to the river Clyde and it is recorded that Port-Glasgow receives on average 14 days more rain in the year than Glasgow itself. It is recorded that it has been frequently remarked the wetter the weather is the healthier the inhabitants are

The River Clyde opposite the parish is supposed to be about

2 miles broad it is only a small part of which is navigable by vessels at burden. This part is called the channel and lies along the new Port-Glasgow shore and is about a two hundred yards broad at average and is so deep at high water that the largest vessels that enter the Clyde can easily be moored in the harbour without discharging any part of the cargo

There are some small cod and haddock in the river opposite to the parish but they are not in such quantities as to render it worth anyone's while to make a trade of fishing. Although Herring make occasional visits but this has only happened 3 times during the previous century.

About the year 1700 the population was about 350 and this gradually increased till the year 1775 when approximately 4,000 people lived in the parish. In recent years the population of the parish has remained stationary and the cause of this was undoubtedly the American war for there is not a port in Britain upon which that event had more immediate influence than upon this port. Glasgow, upon which the people of the New Port-Glasgow chiefly depended, no longer became a commercial but a manufacturing city and consequently no longer the immediate source of wealth to them and with their own internal vigour not being yet sufficiently raised for their support their number could not increase as it had done for nearly a century before.

The better sort of people here are sober, industrious and charitable and are at all times attended to the interests of the poor particularly so in the extraordinary lean years of 1782 and 1783 where they imported large quantities of meal and sold it to the poor at reduced prices cheerfully taking the loss sustained upon themselves. The inferior sorts of inhabitants are a different sort of complexion, sobriety and industry are certainly not their sort of characteristics. It is almost incredible what quantities of spirituous liquors and especially the worst sort of whiskey consumed in this town and it is painful to add that, truth require it, not a little of it is consumed by women. In the town there are no fewer than 81 houses which have a licence for selling ale and spirits besides several others which deal clandestinely in these articles without any licence at all.

In the channel of the river opposite the castle of Newark several pieces of wreck have at different times been discovered. Tradition has it as far back as the memory of the oldest inhabitant now living that when the Spanish Armanda was defeated and dispersed by the English in 1598 and some of the Spanish ships were seen hovering over the west coast of Scotland and so one or more of the vessels were ordered to be sunk in this part of the river to prevent those ships of war should they attempt it from surprising the castle of Dumbarton about 5 miles above this place.

Immediately before you is the river Clyde having all the appearance of a freshwater lake the outlet to the sea is not visible and numbers of large and small vessels are sailing upon it. The opposite coast of Dumbarton and Argyll shores abound in gentlemen's seats, and the crags in the distance are known by the indefatigable name of "the Duke of Argyll's bowling Green".

* * *

Gourock is approximately one third part of the parish of Inverkip and the writings of the reverend Thomas Brown discuss little of particular interest:

The Hereditor of Gourock is a Mr Duncan Darroch who lives in the village which has a population of approximately 400 people. The situation of Gourock is very convenient for trade having sufficient depth of water for vessels of any burden and good shelter. In the village a ropework was commenced in 1777 and succeeds well and employs at present 49 people and manufactures about 165 tons of hemp yearly. There are two mills on this direct estate one for extracting oil from linseed and the other for washing materials belonging to the ropeworks company.

Agriculture in and around the parish has greatly decreased over the past 50 years and many abandoned cottages can be seen. The inhabitants are not gifted in agriculture being more interested in seafaring lives and subsequently moving to places such as Greenock where their employment is based. At this time there is no harbour in Gourock, no landing place other than the beach.

* * *

The town and parish of Greenock on the south side of the Clyde was one of the developments in that area and the report by the reverend Archibald Reid runs to 28 pages.

Greenock was formed into a parish in 1636 when the proprietors appealed to the Lords of Commission for the Plantation of Kirks and the lands were disjoined from Inverkip and Houston and erected into a parish named Greenock. The name Greenock is derived from the Gaelic Grianeg which translates into "the bay of the Sun".

With the exception of a strip of level ground along the waterside the majority of the lands of Greenock were hilly. The lands progressed westward for a distance of about 2 miles when the bay of Gourock forms a boundary, Gourock being part of the parish of Inverkip.

Along the lands adjoining the shoreline which are light and sandy and full of gravel, frequent northern winds blow ashore seaware which manure's the lands which then produce goods crops of oats and barley and very large quantities of potatoes of the best quality but apart from the shoreline lands most of the soil in the parish is thin and bare.

It is interestingly noted that scooping into the rocks a good way above the high water mark a fine polish of the gravel and shells are of the same kind as found on the shore and it is evident that the sea has greatly receded.

It is also recorded that half way between the town of Greenock and Port Glasgow along a public road between the two towns, is Capellow where according to tradition favoured by the name of the place and several ruined habitations, some Dutch fishers long ago resided.

On the west side of the bay of Greenock, which was formerly called "The Bay of St. Lawrence" from a chapel near it dedicated to that saint, in the beginning of the 1700's the habitation consisted of a row of houses covered with thatch along the bay but no harbour whatsoever for vessels. The population of the parish in 1745 did not exceed 4,000 and this decline to about 3,800 by the year 1755. But about the year 1760 the town began to increase rapidly and continued to do so till the American war which occasioned an almost entire stagnation of its trade. Immediately however on the peace of 1783 trade revived and Greenock is now a more flourishing place containing no fewer than 15 thousand people.

The present town of Greenock which is governed by a council is a Burgh of Barony created in the year 1757 by Sir John Shaw who was the then superior. It now embraces the previous village of Cartsdyke which has a good harbour and Quay much older than that of Greenock and was created a Burgh of Barony in 1633 by King Charles the 2nd.

By a sand bank of considerable breadth stretching from Dumbarton to a little below the present town of Greenock the shipping lane is made narrow and navigation to Port Glasgow sometimes tedious and difficult. At low ebbs except for two slanting gaps through it the riverbed is dry and abounds with shellfish of various kinds.

At the western end of the bank or tail as it is usually called is a mooring place where experienced mariners prefer to any other harbour in the Firth and there is at all times sufficient depth of water and abundance of good anchoring ground for hundreds of ships. The development of a harbour was proposed in Greenock and in the year 1700 the Scottish parliament was petitioned for a fund to build it but the petition was absolutely refused by parliament.

Some considerable time after, a contract was entered into with Sir John Shaw the superior and a voluntary contribution of 1shilling and 4d sterling was laid on each sack of malt brewed into ale within the limits of the town and in consequence of this the harbour was begun in 1707 within two circular quays extending to an area of ten acres. The expense was great and the town men alarmed at the greatness of the debt assigned the debt to the superior John Shaw. After the union of Crowns however the trade of the port increased so rapidly than in the year 1740 the whole debt was extinguished and remaining surplus funded the foundation of the town. It may seem extraordinary that relatively minor tax on malt should create such sizeable funds but ale was the only drink of the labouring people and in the year 1792 the number of licensed premises in Greenock was 247.

Before the union of the crowns, merchants of the town had some trade to the Baltic and imported timber in exchange for Herrings together with some trade with France, Spain and other parts of Europe. In the year 1714 a customs house was established at Greenock and a very great trade was carried on principally by the Glasgow merchants who were the owners of almost all the sailing ships calling in that port. The custom's records recall that in 1791 over one thousand ships docked at Greenock bringing from the West Indies rum, sugar, cotton and mahogany and from the Americas rice, Naval stores, potatoes, oil, timber, and from France, Spain and Portugal wines and fruits. The trade to the Baltic for timber and Naval stores is very considerable and the coasting trade is carried on to all the ports of Ireland and the west of England for grain. With the opening of the canal between the forth and Clyde in an extensive trade to the east coast has opened up and also to London and from Greenock are exported Herring, coals and all sorts of British manufactures. From Greenock there are by canal 44 packets to Leith, Dundee and London and to all parts of the Highlands and Isles as far as Orkney and packets to Liverpool fine sloops of 80 tons and upwards well fitted for the accommodation of passengers.

Fishing was a principal force of the wealth of Greenock and it may be proper to mention the reign of Charles the 2nd and under the patronage of the Duke of York a society of Herring fishers was established on the Clyde with particular privileges. At the east of Greenock in 1676 they included a large piece of ground which they called "The Royal Close" for the purpose of curing Herrings. Much later the society was dissolved and the close which was owned by the city of Glasgow merchants has by the time of these writings long been occupied as storehouses for tobacco.

The herring fishery however was continued by individuals and not without success in boats on the rivers and neighbouring lochs and in larger vessels to the isles. A society for the Free British Fishery was established by an act of parliament in the 1750 which granted bounty to fishers for their catches and it is recorded than in the year 1791 at the ports of Greenock and Port Glasgow 53,500 barrels of herrings were landed.

In the neighbouring bays and lochs excellent Salmon are caught in their season and Cod, Haddock and whiting are got in great plenty from the rock of Ailsa upwards with which the ports of Greenock and Port Glasgow supply Glasgow, Paisley and adjacent countryside.

Seaports are not conducive to manufacturing and the population favour a seafaring to a sedentary way of life, but in the year 1725 a ropeworks and sometimes afterwards a sailcloth manufacturing business was established and are now several of them on the river where large quantities of cordage and sailcloth are made for on consumption and exportation.

The minister records with respect to shipbuilding that "it may not be improper" to mention that formerly all the large vessels belonging to the Clyde were built in America but since the Americans established their independence shipbuilding has developed briskly on the ports of the Clyde and the largest merchant vessel ever built in Scotland was launched at Greenock about 1792 belonging to a company in the town who have a contract with the government for supplying the Royal Navy with malts from Nova Scotia.

There was significant nuisance in the town at this time where with the tide rising and falling 10 feet drainage from the town meets the high tide and floods the streets distributing all its blood and filth through the breadth of the town. This shocking nuisance her magistrates and principal people of the town have repeatedly attempted to remove but all their endeavours have been in vain so far.

The mention of one nuisance introduces another which as it give pain to inhabitants and strangers of human feelings ought to if possible be removed. The earnings of the carman who ply the quays are very considerable and the sober among them grow rich but the dissipated drink whisky, rape their families and starve their horses. In about 1780 there was only one stagecoach from Greenock to Glasgow and now in 1793 there 4 every day together with one to Irvine and in winter one between Greenock and Port Glasgow.

And finally it is recorded that the influence of people from all parts means that at many time of the day it is possible to walk from one end of the town to the other passing people without hearing a word of any language but Gaelic.

* * *

Mr John Strutt the minister of the parish of Luss was prolific in his report and indeed produced 34 pages of the most detailed descriptions. Picking out the main points that he makes we note that:

By an act of the Privy Council in 1621 the lands of Buchanan were dislodged from this parish and that later the lands adjoining at Bonhill were dislodged from the parish and in 1658 the lands of Arrochar were detached from it to form a separate parish.

Scarcely one twelth of the parish is arable the greater part being hilly and mountainous but the climate is mild and temperate and snow seldom lies on the low ground. The mountains will protect the force of wind in every direction and the lake never freezes. The area is well known for the longevity of its inhabitants and many reach well into their nineties.

In winter the surface of Loch Lomond has been known to rise 6 feet higher than it is after much drought in summer and its average height above sea level is 22 feet which is considerably higher than it was therefore gaining upon ground. There is some evidence of this particularly in the middle of the Bay of Camfraddan where when the water is low there is a heap of stones to be seen where the Corms of Camfradden were said to have had their family residence. About 5 miles further south and at a distance from the shore there is another heap of stones said to be the ruins of a church. The field opposite is still called the church field. This rise in the surface of the loch has probably been due the mud building up near the mouth of the Leven and damming up the water

There are presently about 30 islands in loch lomond and many of them are finely wooded. Some are inhabited and prove at times formodious asylums to the disordered in mind

Loch Lomond has long been famed for 3 wonders i.e. fish without fins, waves without wind and the floating island. The vipers which are found in the islands are so amphibious as to swim from one island to another are probably the fish without fins. A swelling wave without any wind is not peculiar to the Loch it may be a weatherisium of the great extent of water if a calm immediately succeeds a storm. But independent of any commotion in the atmosphere at the time of the remarkable earthquake in Lisbon in 1755 the waters of Loch Lomond suddenly rose many feet above the former level and this is probably occurrence which caused the substantial damage to Dumbarton referred to in other parts of this book. A small island lying near the west shore is called the floating island is now at least fixed there but has floated down the loch in the process of its creation by clinging together of the matted roots of grasses, willows and light vegetation

There are 880 acres under natural wood and of these about 700 are entirely oak woods which have been cut down every 20 years. The woods are properly divided into 20 separate parts one of which may be cut down every year and the tanins extracted from the trees and used in the textiles processes of the companies in the Vale of Leven. It would appear that the minister was very much interested in natural history and he lists out 102 different birds which are found in the area, which include both ring tailed sea eagles, ospreys, kites and other birds of prey he also lists out 20 animals which includes wild cats, pole cats, pine martins, otters and their like.

The population is 917, which is roughly balanced between males and females and claims that there are 915 members of the established church. Perhaps a little bit of wishful thinking here. He lists occupations as being 76 farmers, numerous smiths, shopkeepers, masons and other tradesmen, 11 weavers, 85 servants, and 120 scholars. The yearly expense of managing a stock of 600 sheep which over a year costs £90 to keep and at the end of the year bringing in a sales value of £115 showing a profit of £25 on the year and he comments that the profit arising from such a flock seems inadequate to the trouble and risk.

In the ownership of property there are 3 heritors, one of whom resides occasionally. Sir James Colquhoun of Luss is proprietor of the greatest part of the lands in the parish the family residence is about 3 miles from Luss on the black promontory or head of land which is finely wooded. There is an excellent modern house there which commands noble views of the lake which was built by the late Sir James Colquhoun

There are 2 slate quarries which between them export from the area over 500,000 slates a year some to Greenock and Glasgow but the greatest part into Stirlingshire.

In 1790 a cotton mill was erected near the village of Luss sufficiently large as to give bread to such as might otherwise be wanting employment but not to encourage the vices which apt to abound where ever a promiscuous multitude of people is assembled. It employees from 30 to 40 hands both young and old.

The language used south from Luss is English and north from Luss the Gaelic the service in the church is performed in both of these and the people in general are sober and industrious and charitable.

* * *

The Reverend Alexander McAulay, minister of the parish of Cardross, notes that in those days the boundary of Cardross was the western bank of the river Leven and the parish stretched along the Clyde for a period of seven miles to its boundary with the parish of Rhu.

Farming has not yet made the progress which might have been expected but it has for the last 10 years been making progress. The main problem seems to have been the prejudice that you should not plough the land before the 10th of march the consequence that growing seasons tend to be missed but these prejudices which stem from some historical beliefs now gradually disappearing.

There are two great roads through the parish the one leading to Loch Lomond, the other running along the Clyde both of which should be kept in the best possible repair. The population has lately greatly increased and there are now 2,194 people in the area of which 251 are employed as hired servants of one description or another

In that part of the parish which is in the Vale of Leven a considerable textile industry grew up some of which some was work being transferred by companies out of the Glasgow area to take advantage of the softness and transparency of the water of the Leven which was particularly fitted to the purpose of bleaching. One company built a significant organisation by 1772 in the area now known as Dalquhurn whereby 1792 the company employed 876 people in the area both in the spinning and weaving mills, pitch works and the print fields where the fabric was laid out to weather.

By the year 1782 the number of people employed in the textile industry had become so numerous the it was extremely difficult to accommodate them in houses and lodgings in the neighbourhood. Mrs Smollett of Bonhill on whose land lay most of the activity, readily embraced the opportunity to improve her family estate and accordingly a village was planned by the advise and the narration of the son now her successor. The new village which was laid out from 1782 onwards was called Renton and consisted of 3 principle streets running in direction from north to south parallel to one another.

There is one distillery in the parish and the number of public houses or rather whisky shops has of late been greatly diminished and justices have of late only given licences to only two in the village of Renton to sell spirits of home produce. There are 3 corn mills and 4 different ferries 2 of these are of great antiquity as appears from the character of the proprietors.

The Yair fishing is so productive in this parish, and seem to be almost peculiar to it. The Yair is the stones gathered from the tide water mark and laid about 4 feet in height for a considerable length out into the river in the form of a crescent. At high tide the fish are swept in behind these closures as the tide goes out a narrow aperture facilitates the netting of the fish which are obtained in great quantities, particularly herrings and also salmon in small quantities during the spring and summer months. Along the tidal shore there are many such enclosures but most are situated in the properties of Mr Dennison of Colgrain and Mr noble of Noble Farm. The rights to these yair fishing's prove themselves to be of very great antiquity being granted by the Crown about 500 years ago and by these the proprietors have the right to exercise yair fishing upon the shore to low water mark plus a distance a man can ride beyond low water and from there throw a 12 foot spear which provides a clear definition where the fishing boats can net and the yair fisherman can use their system.

It has been remarked from the earliest accounts of that kind of fishing that the herrings visit the river Clyde at nearly 3 equal periods within each 100 years each period consisting of several years fishing

A little west of the Leven on a small eminence called Castlehill stood he said a castle at times a residence of King Robert the Bruce. In this castle which no trace is now discernible, a favourite prince of historic tradition breathed his last. A farm in the neighbourhood still pays the supriefeuduty called dogmeal. This tax is supposed to have originally supplied the maintenance of his majesty hounds.

* * *

The Reverend George Drummond writes of the parish of Rosneath whose ancient name was Roffnachoich which is the Gaelic work signifying the virgin's promontory.

The parish is a peninsular with parallel sides being about 7 miles long and 2 miles broad. The higher grounds are covered with heath the lands to the shore are green there is on the promontory a lake a mile in circumference which abounds with perch.

There is good fishing, salmon and herring are caught with nets the other fish such as cod, mackerel and flounders by line. There is a strong current in the Gareloch between the parishes of Rosneath and Rhu opposite where there is a ferry. There are 2 bays on the coast one called Callwattie and the other Campfoil in which there is good anchorage of safe harbour for ships of any burden.

In the Duke of Argyll's park there is a remarkable rock which though now of considerable distance from the shore bears evident marks of having being washed by the sea. It is 34 feet high and is called Wallace's leap from a tradition of the renowned William Wallace being closely pursued by a party of his enemies jumped down this rock on horseback and escaped unhurt but his horse was killed by the fall and was buried at the foot of the rock where his grave is shown.

The population of the parish is 521 and there is the usual spread of craftsmen such as weavers, smiths, shoemakers, tailors and carpenters. It appears that the principal employment is reflected by 48 farmer, 96 herring fishermen and 22 household servants.

There are 98 houses in the parish all of which are detached there being no towns or villages. The decrease of the population over the last 40 years mainly owing to one proprietor having taken into his own possession some farms at which several families formerly lived and partly because some farms are let now to fewer tenants. Yet even at present we are flocked with inhabitants.

There are few ale houses but plenty of whisky houses which are rather unfriendly to the morals of the people. 12 new ale houses have been built within the last 10 years and for each of these except 3 an old house has been pulled down. There are almost no cottagers employed in agriculture unless by the Duke of Argyll. It is difficult to say whether it is better to employ them or hire servants.

Chapter 8   AD 1750 – 1850 Development of Local Estates

Vale of Leven – Loch Lomond – Buchanan Castle – Ardencaple – Rhu – Shandon – Rosneath Peninsular – Coulport.

During this 100-year period many of the estates in the area became owned by people who built on them substantial properties, most of which we can either still see today or are recently recorded.

Covering first the Vale of Leven and Loch Lomond area, we note that John Buchanan, who inherited his father's business in 1789, Glasgow's largest hat factory, and a share in Glasgow's first bank, The Ship Bank, sought to expand his properties along Loch Lomondside by acquiring Little Boturich and Balloch Estate from the Colquhouns in 1802, and Boturich Castle from Haldane of Gleneagles in 1811. These estates are on the lower east side of Loch Lomond, and in 1834 John Buchanan also purchased Poturic Mansion. His son-in-law, Robert Finlay, inherited the property and his descendants still occupy it today.

Being an affable character, John Buchanan allowed the public access to his policies and would readily enter into conversation with them, some of whom would be invited to the Castle for a 'wee Dram'. A frequent visitor was Sir Walter Scott, during the height of his fame. Loch Lomond Castle at Balloch, which stands today in the middle of a park, is currently under a 99-year lease to Dumbarton District Council. Most visitors are surprised to learn that the lochside path is a medieval roadway used by the Lennox nobility and by travellers on the way to and from the pass at Balmaha.

The estate of Ross Priory was at one time part of the Kilmaronich estate of the Cunninghams, from whom it was acquired by Walter Buchanan in 1624. During the period 1810 to 1815 John rebuilt Ross in the romantic style of the period. Sir Walter Scott was a friend of this Buchanan and became a regular visitor here where he learned, in 1817, about Rob Roy's exploits and wrote part of *The Lady of the Lake*.

Cameron House, on the lower west bank of Loch Lomond, currently a luxurious hotel, marina and golf course, was once the property of the Dennistouns of Colgrain. They sold the estates in 1612, and, after a handful of owners, it was ultimately acquired in 1763 by James Smollett, Laird of Bonhill. The estate contained an old 14th century keep which had many tunnels and underground passages. About 1790 the mansion was enlarged, altered in 1806 and subsequently rebuilt after a fire in 1865. It was occupied by the Telfor-Smollett family until its sale to the hotel company in the 1980's.

Across the road is a magnificent mansion currently used as Loch Lomond Youth Hostel which has an interesting history. Originally there were three Achendennan estates, known collectively as Achendennan Rye, or the royal hunting field of King Robert the Bruce during his residency at Cardross. It was gifted to Dumbarton by a religious establishment in the 1500's and was feued out to Sir Andrew Dennistoun. From 1609 it belonged to various branches of the Napier family, and passed through a number of hands, until it was owned by George Martin who built the mansion currently standing in 1864. In his early life, Martin had founded businesses in India, and the Philippines, as well as his native Glasgow, . The buildings were used as a re-habilitation centre in the Second World War. After the war the trade unions of the USA gave a substantial grant to modify it, as the world's then largest youth hostel and conference centre.

On the lochside a few yards further north than the hostel is another property known as Auchendenan-righ, also known as Auchenheglish – the field of the Kirk. The property was used as Lomond Castle Hotel before it was destroyed by fire in 1990. The mansion was built in 1858 by Burnet for the Brock family, one of whose members was the first manager of the Clydesdale Bank. During construction, a turf dyke enclosing a kirk yard was located. The long forgotten burial ground was probably utilised by Clan Colquhoun sometime in the 1600's or 1700's. A few hundred feet offshore are the sunken remains of the kirk which is implicit in the name. Immediately south is an area which used to be an open shore where livestock had access to the drinking water of the loch. It is currently known as Duck Bay, with a marina, hotel and bar.

A little further along the western lochside is the house currently known as Arden, divided into 14 separate apartments. The property standing there today was built in 1868 and was designed again by the same Burnet.

The Act of Union of 1707 allowed Scotland access to English trade routes, an advantage the Scots were not slow to utilise. The tobacco trade played a major part in Glasgow's prosperity in the 1700's. Eventually over half of the UK. total trade in tobacco was controlled by the Glasgow tobacco lords, one of whom was George Buchanan who acquired Auchindennan-Dennistoun in 1770, changing its name to Arden. Buchanan's father had an estate in Virginia which butted the estate of the George Washington family, whose elder brother Lawrence served under Admiral Vernon at the voyage against Carthagena featured by Tobias Smollett in "Roderick Random". The Washingtons and Buchanans named their estates after this admiral, hence Mount Vernon in south-east Glasgow. Sir James Lumsden, who was Lord Provost of Glasgow and knighted by the Prince of Wales in 1868, bought the estate and built the present house.

Further along the western bank of Loch Lomond is the House of Rossdhu, the family seat of the Colquhouns. They owed their first advancement to Malduin, 3rd Earl of Lennox, who granted Unfridus a charter to the lands of Old Kilpatrick. The original castle of Colquhoun was Middleton, north of Milton, but they then moved to Dunglas, on the banks of the Clyde. Subsequently the 4th Laird, Sir Humphrey, obtained a charter for the lands of Luss as reward for his loyalty to The Bruce, and his successor consolidated his inheritance by marrying the Fair Maid of Luss, heiress to the ancient family of Luss, and settled down in a 12th century castle on Eilan Rossdhu, which was replaced in the 1400's by a castle on the mainland. The present mansion was built about 1773 and is currently the clubhouse of the burgeoning Loch Lomond Golf Club. The Laird's wife, Lady Helen, after whom Helensburgh was named, shed a tear when she moved from her lucky home in the old castle to the modern mansion, which her ghost is said to haunt.

Further north from Rossdhu, in a bay, stands a small statue on a plinth 50 or more yards offshore. Many theories and legends abound about its significance, but it may interest the reader to know that this was not a memorial to a drowned child, Colquhoun or otherwise, or as a memory to a wealthy man adopted in his childhood by an Australian to mark the spot of their fortuitous meeting. In fact the statue was erected by a William Kerr, an orphan brought up in Luss, who went to London and made his fortune as a stonemason. The statue was originally intended to be part of a building in Balham, London, but was unwanted by the buyer. It lay in Mr Kerr's yard for quite some time before it was brought to Bandry Bay and erected in 1890. Photographs at that time indicate that the water in the loch was much lower and the party unveiling the statue, which included several elderly ladies, walked out to the point of the statue and posed for their photographs.

Further north than Rossdhu, and just south of Luss, is the ancient town of Camstradden which will be recognised today by the slate quarries on the hillside above. Sunk into the Bay of Camstradden are said to be the many ruins of the old tower and its orchard. The modern mansion of Camstradden was built as a replacement by the 12th Laird in 1739, but by 1868 the ruins were said to be a pile of stones only visible when the water level was low. At one time there was a ford between the mainland and Inchtavannach, but the water level here is now quite deep. The slate quarries on the hillside above date back to the 1500's. At one time they were extremely important for the local economy, the workers being housed in the town of Camstradden, later known as Halfway, until the estate of Camstradden was purchased by the Colquhouns in 1826. This consolidated the growth of the nearby Luss village, where the workers were later housed.

At their peak, in late Victorian times, the quarries employed 30 men, quite apart from the boatmen and labourers who transported the product – 800,000 slates, costing between 15 shillings and two pounds per thousand, were produced annually, mainly for the Glasgow market.

The village of Luss has been in existence since the 1200's, although there appears to be legend that in medieval times the old village of Luss sank into the loch as a result of an earthquake. A pile of stones just offshore, and known as the old church, is offered as proof of this legend. By the 1850's this ancient village, with its picturesque thatched and comfortable cottages, was demolished. A new village had emerged by 1877 around the pier which had existed since 1850, and more modern cottages, as we see them today, had risen from the rubble of the old. The right to hold annual fairs in the village was granted by an Act of Parliament in 1695 whereby the laird of Colquhoun and Luss could stage a weekly market at Luss and full fairs annually, each three days' duration. At one time every family in the village had a boat for fishing on the loch or for hiring to tourists, and it is interesting to note that Luss village enjoyed the privilege of sanctuary (gyrth) granted by Robert the Bruce to his close friend Malcolm, 5th Earl of Lennox, in 1315.

After the 1850's expansion of the village, the old inn was considered inadequate to deal with the increasing population and the tourists who were discovering Loch Lomond. The Loch Lomond and Trossachs tour was gaining popularity – this entailed travelling by steamer up Loch Katrine, then by coach to Inversnaid to catch the Loch Lomond steamers. The passengers disembarked at will, Luss being a popular stop. The Colquhoun Arms, originally a small drovers' inn, was expanded in 1860 on the outskirts of the village, and a map of the military road drawn up by Taylor and Skinner in 1776 shows the old inn with the road leading diagonally down to Luss Kirk. Most of the deliveries to the hotel were made by steamer and it was a welcoming sight to the locals to see them unloading barrels of beer which were then rolled up Pier Road to the hotel, the focal point of village social life.

Travelling north from Luss, we come across the Inverbeg Inn which was based amongst a number of shielings scattered along the promontory shore of Inverbeg, called Lower Inverglus in those days. The Ferry Inn of Inverbeg was built about 1814 and was a focal point for travellers to the north and the ferry across from Rowardennan.

Further north and approaching Tarbet, Loch Lomond, the lands of Stuckgowan (meaning new oak cottage) were granted to the son of MacFarlan until 1739, when they were sold to a Mr Syme. Towards the end of the 1700's the estate was acquired by the McMurrich clan, when Mureach, a descendant of an Irish King, reclaimed about 50 acres of the rocky and woody wilderness above Stuckgowan and built a regency gothic villa, which is now a listed building. Nowadays the property is owned by Luss Estates and is run as a hotel. The grounds contain some remarkable arboreal specimens, a Monterey pine 120 feet in height, and the largest redwood in Scotland, 150 feet. About 500 yards or so south-west on the hillside are the ruins of the "Black Village" whose inhabitants were wiped out by a plague in the 1600's

Further north at Tarbet, where the road divides to Crianlarich and to Arrochar, there has been a coaching inn since 1570. The current frontage to the hotel was built in 1882, and was known as the Colquhoun Arms. In 1904 the Tarbet Hotel Company was formed to look after the interest of the establishment and a further extension was added in 1974. Until the 1930's there was a horse coach service between Tarbet and Arrochar to link to the Glasgow steamers. Therefore, it was possible to sail up Loch Lomond, coach to Arrochar and sail back down Loch long and then on to Glasgow.

About 100 yards north of the hotel there is the hill called "Still Brae". A building currently there was erected in 1745 as a distillery.

Local grain was used in the whisky production, which was exported out of the locality. Window tax made glass rather costly, causing the closure of the distillery due to lack of bottles. Since those days the building has housed an undertaker, a joiner, a plumber and a weaver.

Arrochar, which means "hilly country", was named after the parish of the same name which for five and a half centuries was the patrimony of the Clan Macfarlane. The Cobbler Hotel is built on the site of the clan chief's castle of Inverioch. The community used to mainly be a crofting one.

In 1825 the Rev. Peter Proudfoot, minister at Arrochar, was receiving complaints about the distance his congregation from the northern parts of his parish had to travel to attend a service. So the congregation at Ardlui on Loch Lomond hewed out the face of the 28,000 ton "Pulpit Rock", an opening large enough to hold a minister, an elder and a presenter. The vestry was reached by a flight of steps and had a wooden door, and for about 70 years services were held on a monthly basis during the summer, usually with a congregation of about 100, who sat on turf on the ground around the rock.

Inversnaid Hotel, on the east bank of Loch Lomond, which can only be reached by water or over the hills behind it, was not built on the site of the mansion of Rob Roy, as in popular legend. Inversnaid proper is about one mile inland, and the site of Rob's house was about one mile north-east of the hotel, on the west bank of the Snaid Burn. The buildings, which became the current Inversnaid Hotel, were originally a hunting lodge and a ferryman's cottage. These were developed to become the hotel about 1820.

Situated approximately one mile north of Inversnaid is a large cavern known as Rob Roy's cave. This large cavern with a small opening was originally called Bruce's cave after the Scottish patriot, who while being chased by his enemies sought shelter there. On entering the cave, the Bruce heard the sound of breath and thought he had fallen into a trap, but the breathing belonged to some wild goats and not to his enemies. The goats were a godsend, for by snuggling up to them he had a warm and comfortable night, and was so grateful that he granted these goats royal protection. Four centuries after Bruce's time Rob Roy would use this cavern as a place of concealment with about 20 of his men. From here he held his levies, summoned councils of war and arranged methods of collecting revenue for supplies.

Very nearby, not to be confused with the more famous Rob Roy's Cave, is a rock which rises sharply from the lochside to a height of 30 feet. It has a flat top from which projects another steep rock of greater height. From here it was said Rob Roy would fix a rope round the waist of his adversaries, creditors and debtors and proceed to dump them in the loch below. Those who would refuse his demands were let down again, but this time with a subtle hint that, if they remained stubborn and did not agree to his terms, the rope would be tied round their necks. Rob Roy invariably got the settlement he asked for.

Further south on the east bank of Loch Lomond is the Rowardenan Hotel, site of a hostelry since at least 1696, when the current charter was granted by the 3rd Marquis of Montrose to create a droving inn and a houlth, a place of sustenance and refreshment. The hostelry remained in the hands of the Duke of Montrose and family until acquisition by the Montrose estates in 1926. Charles M. Collins, of the famous Glasgow-based publishing company, brought the property in 1931 and it continued to be developed as a hotel.

The western half of Ben Lomond was part of Rob Roy Macgregor's Inversnaid and Craigroystan estates, of nearly 7,000 acres which he acquired in 1693. They contained about 900 people, living in long-gone clachans. At the beginning of the 1800's, Sir James Colquhoun invited Sir John Murray Macgregor, both being clan leaders, to Rossdhu where they visited the Glen Fruin battle site and shook hands in reconciliation, as the two clans had been feuding for centuries.

The Highland boundary fault line which extends from Stonehaven to Helensburgh, passes through Loch Lomond at Balmaha on the east shore and Arden on the west. The pass of Balmaha is a rugged and steep defile, and during droving days was the gateway to the highlands. At the foot of the pass was an old tollhouse, or "passfoot", which has since been altered and extended. Two and a half miles north of Balmaha, at Strathcashel Point, are the ruins of the iron age fort of Cashel, offshore from which, when the water level is low, can be seen the wooden beams of a cranog,s built around the same time.

Adjacent to the village of Drymen is Buchanan Castle, best known nowadays for its ruined Victorian mansion (originally described as the castle), a golf course and extensive executive housing built in the grounds. Supposed to be descended from a son of the Kings of Ulster, who landed in Argyll around 1016, a warrior named Anselan was granted the lands of Buchanan by Malcolm the 2nd as reward for his services against the Danes. The Buchanans were later given the privilege of holding courts of life and limb on their estate by the Earls of Lennox, provided that any execution be carried out on the gallows of Catter, near Drymen, one of the chief Lennox seats.

After 600 years on Loch Lomondside, the Buchanans lost their lands due to the death in 1682, without heir or will, of the 22nd Laird. The lands were acquired by the 3rd Marquis, later Duke, of Montrose who moved here. A later Duke employed the famous gardener Capability Brown to landscape the estate with rich woodlands. The old Buchanan house of 1724 was burned down during Christmas 1852, and by 1854 the ruined mansion was rebuilt. Rudolf Hess, during his mission to the United Kingdom, was received there in 1941. The building is now a ruin, because, it is rumoured, the roof was taken after the Second World War to avoid rates.

Since the advent of easier and more available travel, Loch Lomond has become a romantic attraction for tourists. The first steamer to ply the loch was David Napier's P.S. Marian in 1817, a flat-bottomed wooden boat, 60 feet by 13 feet, and with a funnel almost as tall as the boat was long. Daily at 6 am the P.S. Postboy would leave Glasgow for Dumbarton to connect via a coach up the Vale of Leven with Marian's 10 am sailing. The return trip would arrive in Glasgow at 8 pm. A number of steamers were developed, and in the 1840's the Waterwitch, built locally at Pollochro, was a general-purpose cargo vessel carrying wood to be made into bobbins at the Paisley mills. She sailed via the Leven, navigable at that time, and the Cart, bringing coal on the return trip.

In 1792 James Stirling bought Tullichewan estate from the Colquhouns and erected a castle of "Gothic picturesque", designed by Lugar. James Stirling came to the area when the family firm of William Stirling and Sons, textile printers, established in 1750 in Maryhill in Glasgow, moved to Renton, because of the purer water of the River Leven. It set up the Corderdale Printfield Works above Dalquhourn in 1762 and the United Turkey Red Company in 1770, both prosperous ventures which helped to establish the town of Renton. Later Tullichewan estate was acquired by William Campbell who, with his brother Sir James, former Lord Provost of Glasgow, had founded the firm of J and W Campbell. A son of Sir James, Sir Henry Campbell Bannaman, became Prime Minister, 1902 to 1905.

The lands of Kilmahew in Cardross were granted to John Napier at the end of the 1200's by Malcolm, 5th Earl of Lennox. Within the estate a church was known to exist some time before 1370, and Kilmahew Church was rebuilt by Duncan Napier in 1467. For two centuries it served as the local school. The now-ruined 15th century tower house, a mile east of Cardross village, was built by George Napier, one of the 18 generations of Napier who enjoyed ownership of the estate. Various portions were frittered away, until in 1820 the Napiers lost possession. James Burns of Bloomhill, who had set up a steam navigation business in 1824 with his youngest brother George, acquired Kilmahew about 1858 . His son John, who built Kilmahew mansion, now in ruins, was one of the founders of the Cunard line.

Coming closer into Helensburgh from the southern end we come to Ardmore Point, very likely once an island, a massive quartz-studded pudding-stone rock, thrusting into the Firth of Clyde with sea caves around the higher rock area confirming the previous higher level of the water in the firth.

There was a laird's house on the hill of Ardmore as far back as 1654. The mansion we presently see was built in 1806 by General Thomas Geils. There are three towers within the structure which may date from the 15th or 16th centuries. Behind the house are the splendid remains of a telescopic lookout tower, consisting of three concentric circles, the inner two of local stone, the central portion still housing a spiral stair.

Moving in towards what is now Helensburgh, we come to Camis Eskan which dates from 1648, although it was much remodelled in 1840 and 1915. The house belonged to the Dennistoun family who transferred ownership in 1836 to Colin Campbell of Breadalbane. It became briefly a tuberculosis sanatorium and geriatric hospital, but in the 1970's was converted into luxurious apartments.

Nearby, predating Helensburgh itself and still in position, is Drumfork House, dating from 1748. A studious, two storey house with few architectural pretensions, it lies on the ancient drove road from Loch Lomondside to Drumfork Ferry, where cattle were shipped to Greenock.

Ardencaple Castle was originally built and subsequently developed by the McAuleys, descended from one of the sons of Alwyn 2nd Earl of Lennox in the 1200's. When they built their first castle at Ardencaple it was sited on a promontory with the sea on two sides, thus confirming the legend that the water levels of the Clyde were much higher centuries ago. The castle was rebuilt in the 1500's during Walter McAuley's chiefdomship, and the clan, under his successor Sir Auley, was at the peak of its prosperity. They were feudal landlords with properties extending from Garelochhead to Cardross. After the Glen Fruin massacre the McAuleys turned their backs on the Macgregors in order to escape conviction. For the next century and a half the family fortunes declined and various portions of their estates were sold off. The last Laird of McAuley sold Ardencaple Castle to the 4th Duke of Argyll when the roof fell in and he took refuge in his castle at Faslane. Inevitably Faslane, too, was sold off to the Campbells and the now- landless laird took shelter at High Laggerie above Rhu, where he died in 1767.

Ardencaple was extended by Lord Fredrick Campbell, and, after a fire in 1830, the 7th Duke of Argyll rebuilt the castle in the form in which it remained until Sir James Colquhoun took possession in 1862. It became McAuley's property again, albeit briefly, in the 1920's, when Mrs McAuley-Stromberg acquired it. After its use during the Second World War by the Admiralty, it was demolished in 1957 and only a square tower remains. It was left to form a navigational aid and houses navigational lights. The seawall bastion still remains in a modern housing development.

After the conversion of Napier's mansion at Shandon into a hydropathic centre in the 1880's, the area became an attractive proposition for the well-to-do of the Glasgow society. A ribbon development of mansions and villas sprang up along three miles of coastline. At one time the inhabitants had the cheapest gas lighting in Scotland, supplied from the Helensburgh gas works. A pier was built in 1886, opposite the Shandon Church, now converted into apartments. The pier was closed down in 1967, but it is worth noting that the Gareloch only seven miles in length once boasted eight piers.

To the north of Faslane cemetery, and behind the recently developed by-pass road leading up to Whistlefield, was the 12th century Faslane Castle. It was impregnable, being in the junction between two deep glens. This was one of the strongholds of the Earls of Lennox. William Wallace arrived there to a warm welcome from Malcolm, 5th Earl of Lennox, after destroying Rosneath Castle. By 1543, the castle was bestowed upon Adam Colquhoun who feued portions of the estate, and in 1693 it was attached to the Ardencaple estate of the McAuleys, descended from the early Lennox Earls. No trace of Faslane Castle has existed since the railway was laid through to Garelochhead. Faslane Chapel, dedicated St. Michael, was probably built in the 1300's by the Earls of Lennox for their own use, and the future husband of Mary Queen of Scots, Lord Darnley, whose family inherited the Lennox estates after the partition of the Earldom, was said to have been baptised in the chapel, which stands in the current Faslane Cemetery.

Over the hill, past Whistlefield and on to Loch Long is Portincaple, north of which lived whalers at Glen Malon. In the days before the building of the Rest and Be Thankful road through Glencoe by General Wade in 1768, Portincaple was of strategic importance for travellers to and from Argyll. Drovers coming from Argyll would bring their cattle to Mark Cottage where they were forced to swim across to Portincaple and onwards to Whistlefield, where a drover's inn was situated.

The barony of Rosneath (rhos noeth – the bare or unwooded promontory) belonged in the 1100's to one of the sons of Alwin, the 2nd Earl of Lennox,. Through his marriage to Lady Eva, a daughter of Gilchrist, Earl of Monteith, the estate passed into the Monteith ownership sometime during the reign of David the 1st, 1124 – 53. The castle was built by Alwyn's son early in the 1100's and destroyed by William Wallace towards the end of the 1200's.

When the Campbells of Argyll took possession of the estate by royal grant in the 1400's they re-built the castle. They later enlarged it in 1630. The 5th Duke of Argyll created castelations and other improvements in 1784. After this ancient pile burned down in 1802, the 5th Duke employed the services of Joseph Bonomi, the Elder, to rebuild the castle during the period 1803 – 1806. Princess Louise, a daughter of Queen Victoria, acquired the estate through her marriage to the Marquis of Lorne, heir to the Dukedom of Argyll, in 1871. As she died without issue, the estate was sold after her death in December 1939. After use as military quarters during the Second World War, the castle became unsafe and was blown up in 1961.

The parish of Rhu gained its independence in 1648, when McAulay of Ardencaple offered to finance the construction of a small church and manse. The site lay along the curve of the bay south of the shingle stretch at the mouth of the Gareloch, hence Rhu – from the Gaelic Rhdue, meaning a promontory.

The first thatched shore cottages have long-since disappeared, but the Rhu Inn remains. The first major house in the area was Ardenconnel, built in 1790 for Andrew Buchanan, a Glasgow merchant, who brought the estates in the neighbouring Lettrowalt and Blairvaddick from the luckless McAulays of Ardencaple. This house remains within substantial grounds and is now divided into a number of apartments.

Rhu Point, the unpredictable narrows between Rhu and Rosneath, created the illusion that the banks were within striking distance of each other. They were deepened and widened with the advent of the Trident nuclear submarine base in the 1990's when much blasting and rock removal took place. In the heyday of Dumbarton horse and cattle fairs, animals brought from Argyllshire to Rosneath would circumvent the 10 miles trip around the head of the loch by crossing the short stretch of water. Rhu Point served as a pasture, being called 'ferry acres'. The bleak and unpromising aspect of this grazing ground lay unrealised until 1849 when a mansion, Rosslea, was completed and a plantation of fir trees installed. Rosslea is now a hotel.

The neighbouring Ardenvohr, built in 1858, has lost its extensive hot houses and slated tower, but is currently used as headquarters of the Royal Northern and Clyde Yacht Club.

The Garelochside area of Shandon was originally one of the ancient strongholds of the Earls of Lennox (Sean-dun is Gaelic for old fort, the origin of the name Shandon). Modern Shandon threads its way along the shores of the Gareloch, from the outskirts of Rhu to Faslane bay. The road was widened and re-routed in 1969, with some sections of the old lochside road still remaining, particularly at the southern end of Faslane submarine base.

The whole hillside became covered with substantial houses, the most noteworthy being West Shandon, built in 1852 for Robert Napier, the well-known engineer, to house his collection of books, art works and exotic plants. In the art gallery were hung paintings by Rembrandt, Rubens and Raphael, and the extensive garden ponds and greenhouses were cultivated with rare species, brought to Shandon by the famous explorer David Livingstone. After Napier's death in 1876, the mansion was sold and opened as Shandon Hydropathic Spa, complete with Russian, Turkish and saltwater swimming baths. Prosperity failed to return after the First World War, and the grounds were finally cleared in 1960 as part of the development of the Clyde Submarine Base. A beautiful lodge and the original garden wall, with one extant bartizan, remain on the old shore road, adjacent to the south entry to the Faslane base.

Just north of West Shandon lies the Bay of Faslane. It was formerly a bay of considerable beauty which James the 4th once used as a base for his fledgling navy, attracted by the depth of water and shelter afforded by the surrounding hills.

Faslane was absorbed by the Royal Engineers, as Military Port Number One, during the Second World War and used principally for the shipment of men and materials to the North African and Normandy campaigns. The ground where the submarine ship lift now stands was transformed into a railway marshalling yard, adjacent to six, five hundred foot deepwater berths, 27 cranes and a floating dry dock. At this time a link was taken from the West Highland railway line and run along the dockside. After the war the area was used for many years as a ship breaking facility, scrap metal being taken away by a railway. This continued until the late 1980's when the area was merged into the developing submarine base. The submarine base one sees today was, until the mid 1960's, merely a landing jetty off the old road along the lochside. It serviced HMS Maidstone, which was used as a mothership for the submarine fleet, there being relatively minimal naval development on the land side.

Beyond Faslane lies Garelochhead which straddles the ancient boundaries of Rhu and Rosneath, and consists of a semi- circular clutch of cottages and villas at whose pier no fewer than six different steamers called regularly during the summer seasons of the early 1850's. Development since this heyday has been minimal, although the building of the West Highland railway line, which brought a station and stationmaster's house, did prolong some of the activity in the area.

The road from Garelochhead continues onto the Rosneath peninsular and comes first to Mambeg and Rahane, two hamlets about a mile or so apart. They grew quickly to their present size, one owing to the existence of a small steamboat pier, which closed in 1935, the other, at the foot of the Mill Burn, survived in a whirl of white-washed cottages on Shore Road, including the now restored Mill of Rahane and Old Ferryman's Cottage. Next came Clynder. Until 1817 when the first feu of the Barremman estate was taken up, the east side of the Rosneath peninsular was largely unpopulated. Great vistas of the Firth of Clyde are revealed at the end of the peninsular of Rosneath, no longer the bare, unwooded promontory that gave rise to the Gaelic name Rhosnoeth, now a leafy peninsular.

The estate embracing the end of the peninsular was granted by the King to the Campbells of Argyll in 1459. Their original castle was destroyed by fire in 1802 and replaced by John, 5th Duke of Argyll, with a mansion in 1806. The style in question, whilst betraying the Italian origins of the architect, was more properly neo-classical. These elements combined to shape a Ducal Palace whose elegance was unrivalled in the West of Scotland. However. the house remained unfinished and was sold on the death of Princess Louise, Dowager Duchess of Argyll, in 1939. After use as the administrative centre for the American naval base on Rosneath during the Second World War, the building was abandoned, to be ignominiously blown up in 1961. All that can be seen today is the caravan park sprawling above the shores of Camsail Bay.

Rosneath Home Farm, an integral part of the estate, built in 1803, was a gothic curiosity, three sides of an octagon, beneath a vast, tiled roof and towering steeple, regrettably now an envelope of corrugated iron following a fire.

Princess Louise, the Dowager Duchess of Argyll, while living at

Rosneath Castle, was continuously moving around the area. In 1896 at Rosneath, the Ferry Inn, designed by Henry Lutyens, was constructed on Rosneath Point to facilitate her movements. It was built with substantial suites and a ballroom, at the point where the ferry from Ardencaple/Cairndhu docked. It was a magnificent creation, but, after years of use by the American Navy during the Second World War, the interior was gutted and the whitewashed Ferry Inn Cottage of today was created out of the remaining rear half of Lutyens' inn.

The shoreline of the Rosneath Peninsular is covered with substantial mansions of various types which reflect the enthusiasm of the late 1800's for seaside villas as an alternative to city dwelling. The characteristics of these villas are too numerous to mention in a work of this nature but many are the work of Alexander 'Greek' Thomson. Originally they were dependent on the ferry services linked to Kilcreggan.

Just as Kilcreggan and Cove owe their existence to the arrival of the steamship, so the demise of its popularity signalled an end to the development on the lower western fringe of the Rosneath Peninsular. Its inaccessibility has preserved architectural integrity due to the lack of further development.

Kilcreggan, originally a series of small farms and cottages dependent on the ferry service to Rosneath Inn, was developed on a more speculative basis than Cove, and a pattern-book architectural style emerged. It became something of a social competition to see who could build the biggest house, many of which were loosely described as castles.

Arguably the most interesting property in this area is Knockderry Castle, and said to have been built in 1855 on the dungeons of an ancient Norwegian or Danish lookout tower, dated probably from the time of the battle of Largs in 1266. It is magnificently poised on the edge of a rocky outcrop. It was spectacularly enlarged to the rear in 1896 by William Lieper. Its bulk gives little hint of the delightful

2a, b – Remains of Malig Mill in Hermitage Park (above and below)

3 – Plan of Helensburgh 1864

4 – View down the Clyde from Erskine to Dumbarton Rock c.1830

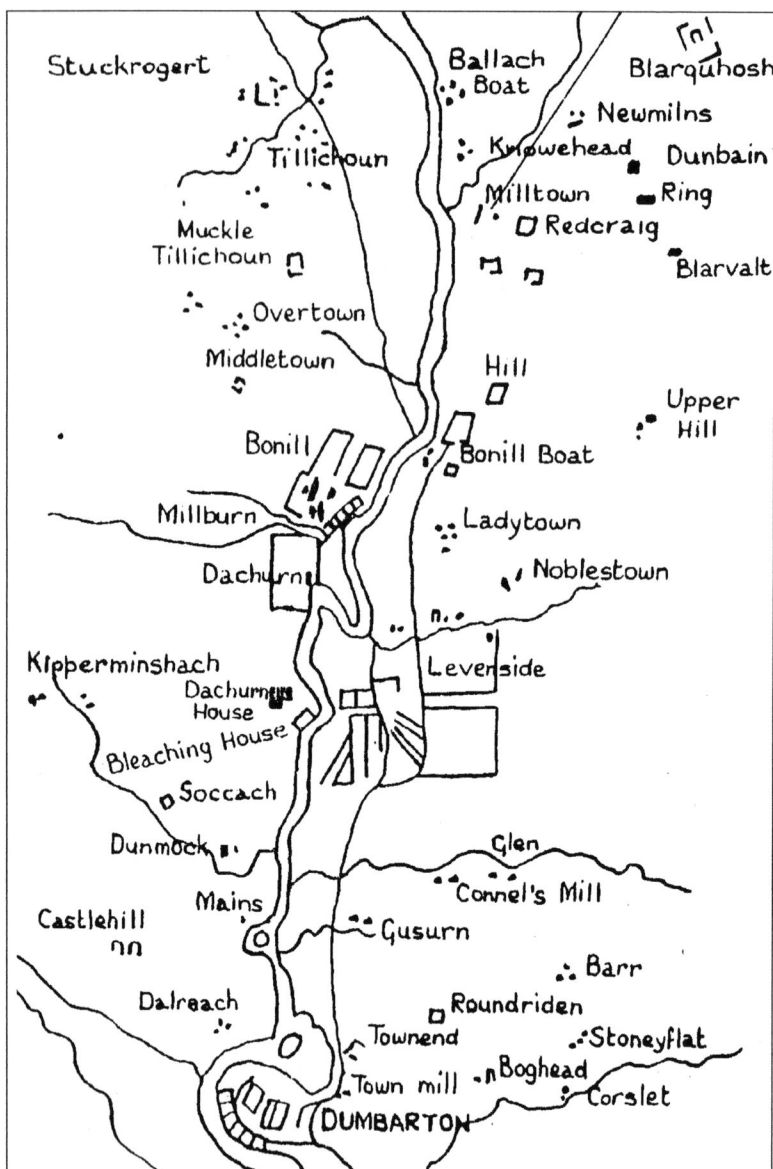

5 – Map of the Vale of Leven c.1750

6 – Helensburgh Pier and Seafront c.1870

7 – Boats beached at Helensburgh c.1830

8 – Helensburgh Pier 1898

9 – Glen Fruin – Strone Farm the site of the 1603 Colquhoun/McGregor Battle

10 – Helensburgh Town Council inspecting the waterworks 1896

11 – Ardencaple Castle – 1930

12 – Helensburgh Seafront 1930

13 – The first car registered in Dunbartonshire – owned in 1910 by Francis Buchanan of Rhu on the Loch Lomondside road

14 – Ariel view of Helensburgh 1966

15 – The lower east corner of Colquhoun Square in 1960

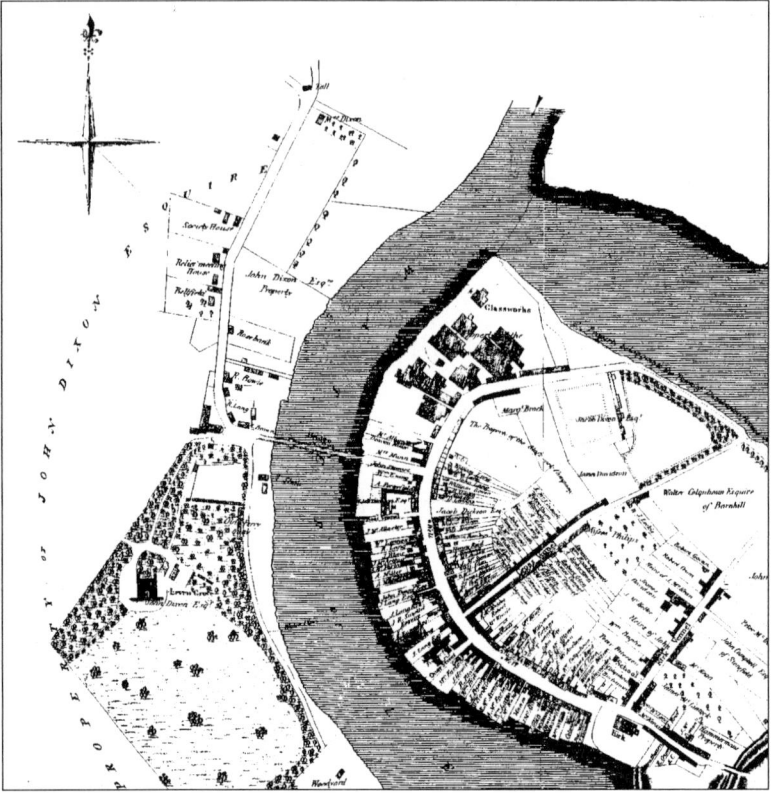

16 – Town Plan of Dumbarton 1818

17 – Ariel view of Helensburgh and Rhu 1998

interior. Inside is a water-powered lift, installed for carpet manufacture and weaver John Templeton, and a glorious banqueting hall in blue and gold, complete with minstrel gallery and frieze. It is within the author's memory that this was run as a hotel. Dining in the banqueting hall and drinking in the dungeons bar was certainly possible in the mid 1970's, although latterly it has become a family home.

A little further north is the area which was originally known as the bay of Coulport. In post-war years it was cleared for the development of a naval armaments establishment. All that remains is an old tin Kirk and a few two storey sandstone villas. Lost in the demolition in the 1960's was John Kibble's Coulport House, built in 1860 as an Italianate mansion with round-headed windows and touches of elegant ironwork.

John Kibble, photographer, astronomer, botanist and greenhouse constructor, built two conservatories onto the house, the larger, reputably costing £15,000, was donated to Glasgow's botanical gardens, towed upriver in 1872 and re-erected with the addition of a huge dome. John Kibble died at Coulport House in 1894 and is best remembered in an area of the botanical gardens known as Kibble Gardens, with its lovely glass and iron conservatory.

Over the hill and down onto Loch Long is Finnart, the fair and beautiful headland marking the boundary between the Highlands and the Lowlands. Here John, Duke of Argyll, erected a tablet commemorating the 1787 construction of the road from Rosneath to Arrochar, still the main route in this area. It passes a magnificent wooded shore which became British Petroleum's first deepwater terminal in 1951. It was built to accommodate tankers bringing crude oil from the Middle East, unloaded, then be piped 57 miles underground to Grangemouth refinery.

Chapter 9   AD 1800 – 1850.

Burgh of Barony – Early Growth – Henry Bell – Distilling – Trading Activities – Robert Napier – Developments in Greenock – James Watt – Canals – Ferry Boats – Railway Development

The proprietor of the new town, John, the 16th laird of Colquhoun, wished to obtain a charter erecting the village into a Burgh of Barony. In a document of March 1802 he recalled his previous development such as it was:

> I had established a village called Helensburgh that there was a convenient market place in the said village and several necessary accommodations for the purpose of giving encouragement to trade, industry and manufacture. Which were carried out there on a considerable extent, that as it might enable me more effectively to accomplish these purposes if the said village, were with some territory around it, erected into a free and independent Burgh of Barony

He envisaged that it would obtain the grant of a weekly market with four annual "fayres". On the 28th July, 1802, a Royal Charter was issued by King George the Third, giving the town a crest, including "the Colquhoun saltire with hound and stag happily combined, and with the three stars and savage of the Sutherland branches of the proprietor's family". For the first time the boundaries of the new town were officially delineated. Bounded on the south by the River Clyde, it extended as far north as the march dykes of Stuckleckie, Milligs and Glennan farms. On the west it was separated from Eastertoun of Ardencaple by the Glennan burn. The eastern boundary was the road leading to Loch Lomond, the Duke's road, as a note of 1792 has it "made by the Duke of Argyll for the convenience of travelling from Rosneath to Inverary before the road by Loch Long was formed".

The burgh was to have a Provost, two Bailies and four Councillors, elected by a general meeting of all the feuers and burghers.

The first council of which we have record met in 1807. Henry Bell was provost, Robert McHutcheon and Thomas Craig, were bailies, and the four councillors were Daniell Colquhoun, Donald McFarlane, John Bramander and Charles Colquhoun. John Gay was town clerk and Robert Colquhoun his deputy.

The council had few of the powers it would have today. It levied the tolls and dues for the weekly market on Thursdays and the four annual fayres, the 2nd Tuesday of February for horses, the 1st of June, 6th of August and the 12th of November for fat cattle and sheep. One of its first enactments was that the times of these should be published in newspapers and handbills, and inserted in the Town Almanac. Plans for a market were passed by a majority on the 19th of February, 1808 but the annual fayres did not bring the hoped-for prosperity to the town, to judge from the fact that the revenues from them were knocked down to one R. McNeil for the princely sum of five shillings.

The burgh's powers under the charter were not all clearly laid down, and in 1845 it was necessary to seek counsel's opinion. The opinion was that the council was entitled to make by-laws for repairing and cleaning the streets and for removing nuisances and dunghills – there were plenty of these in the middle of the century! A procurator fiscal could be legally appointed to bring defaulters before magistrates to pass sentence. Justice was dealt out in primitive fashion and was administered by the bailies. They often sat in Jamie Colquhoun's change house at the Old Granary to try delinquents. The fines imposed were sometimes, it is alleged, converted into aquavitae, punished "by the court and the panels who stood at the bar for the good of the hoose". On one occasion, two worthies, charged with fighting with each other, were taken before one of the bailies who sat in a room of the above-named pub. The bailie berated the officers soundly for bothering with such a trifling case and advised the fighting men that, if they had not punished each other sufficiently and to their hearts content, just to go outside into a quiet corner and finish the job – and he hoped they would be wiser men after.

With the small population of the town, it is perhaps little wonder that there were insufficient volunteers to take up the offices offered under the Burgh of Barony. Fines were drawn up for people who did not take up a position when offered. The "offenders" often preferred to pay a fine of 10 shillings or five shillings rather than accept the office.

Anyone visiting Helensburgh in 1820 would have found only one long row of houses in Clyde Street, small two-storey buildings, none of which exist today, and about half a dozen newly-built ones in Princes Street. There was no esplanade or sea wall, and the old crumbling pier jutted out into the waters of the Clyde. A considerable expanse of grass lay between the road and the beach in the east bay on which schoolboys played their favourite game of shinty. A similar field lay in the front of the west bay and this was usually selected by the itinerant Punch and Judy shows and other travelling showmen. The tide has gradually swept away these two verdant strips of ground, but until the 1970's The Old Granary still reared its unadorned walls where it had stood for so long.

The West or Glennan Burn flowed into the sea close to where William Street now is, a limpid stream, with grassy banks and mossy stones and ferns beautifying its course. It ran into the sea under a humpback stone bridge over which carried the track. On the eastern side of the burn stood the house of Lady Augusta Claverling, built in 1804, and still standing behind what has become Augusta Lodge Café. On the western side of the burn, on Neddy's Point, was the Old Ferry House which doubled as a public house. It was a small, red tiled building with a massive iron ring on each side of the door to which the ferry boat could be attached.

Over the Glennan Burn bridge, the track led to what is now Camsail Avenue, the entrance to the new mansion of Mr Kidson, at Fernigair, the gates of which were originally the start of the avenue to

Ardencaple Castle, where there used to be a picturesque old gate lodge with thatched roof and rustic wooden pillars. It had to be pulled down for the building of Fernigair.

Ardencaple woods, which surrounded the castle, extended to the end of Clyde Street and were full of fine lofty trees. To the east of these woods and Fernigair, mansions were beginning to be developed in an area which was still some way from the town itself.

In the early 1800's the Ardencaple Inn was built by the Duke of Argyll, and the old Cairndhu Inn demolished. Much of its stonework was used in the construction of the stable of the new inn, one of the stages where horses were changed on the coaching run from Glasgow to Inverary. Here, visitors to the Argyll family, at either of their residences, put up their private carriage and horses at what was a bustling and thriving place in the old coaching days.

By around the 1870's its use as an inn was discontinued and it became Mrs Drew's private mansion, although sometime in the early 1900's it again reverted to being an hotel.

In the early 1800's the green fields extended all the way down the slopes to Clyde Street, except in that portion of Princess Street around Colquhoun Square. The east and west burns, apart from the two stone bridges in Clyde Street, were either spanned by small wooden stretchers or crossed by stepping stones. Even in later periods the streets now running up from Clyde Street, with houses and villas on both sides, were merely indicated by incipient side walks and rows of trees, as formalised roads had not been constructed. Around this time there was an hotel, currently is named the Imperial, which stands adjacent to the pier. In the early 1800's this was known as The Tontine Hotel, one of the earliest coaching inns of the town.

The name Tontine was not unique, there being one or two other such hotels, including one in Greenock,. The name derived from the 18th century Italian, Lorenzo Di Tonti, and was used to describe a type of financial arrangement whereby a project was financed by subscribers making a loan from which each was to receive for life an annuity. This was increased as other subscribers died until the last survivor received the whole sum of annuities. It would appear that this was the basis for funding construction of what is now the Imperial Hotel.

At the end of the 1700's the only place of worship for the inhabitants of Helensburgh was the parish church at Rhu. The oldest place of worship in the town was the square building known as the Tabernacle, erected on the site of the present Congregational Chapel in James Street as far back as 1802. This remained for many years the only chapel in Helensburgh. The early Scottish Congregationalists made Helensburgh a preaching station in summer and conducted their services either in or out of doors, according to the state of the weather. Thus a small flock was formed and in 1800 an application was made to the Reverend Greville Ewing to send down from Glasgow some of the young men then studying for the university under his training.

In 1801 subscriptions were gathered to defray the expense of a humble place of worship, without flooring but with a foot board laid on the earth within each pew. A contemporary recollection records that the building itself stood in the middle of a field, where a number of sheep grazed in summer. In wet weather the approach to the building was somewhat difficult for the ground was mossy and undrained and a row of stepping stones led across the line of the then unformed street. Inside, the building was bleak and bare, with high pews all overlooked by an enormous pulpit with a wooden canopy.

Having noted the slow start that the embryonic town had, it is generally acknowledged that the it really began to grow and develop its connections with the Colquhoun family when Sir James, the 18th baronet, who was born in 1804, succeeded to the estates in 1836. Until then it was little more than a village, only growing in importance during his lifetime. Sir James did not cope with popularity and was a retiring and rather reserved man with strangers, but affable and courteous with those he knew more intimately. He was highly esteemed as a landlord and the area was much improved by his liberal and generous outlay on farmsteadings, reclamation and other works. In politics, he was a keen Liberal and for several years represented the County of Dumbarton in Parliament. He was also Lord Lieutenant of the county.

He was a thorough churchman of the old school, and held strong views on Sunday observance. In 1859, when the first Sunday steamer began to ply on the Clyde and the solitude of the Garelochside was broken by Sabbath trippers, he assembled a considerable number of his retainers and resisted the landing of passengers at Garelochhead. A free fight was the consequence and a number of combatants were severely injured. He afterwards raised an action in the Supreme Court, contending, and winning, the point that, as the pier was erected on his private ground and was not in any sense a free pier, he had a right to regulate the traffic. The case excited considerable popular interest.

During his life, the town rapidly increased and the building trade was prosperous. He was helpful in its advancement, for, although a somewhat strict landlord, he was always liberal in gifts of ground or any scheme or public utility. His died on New Year's day, 1874. He had crossed from Rossdhu to Inchlonaig, an island on Loch Lomond, famous as a deer reserve, on a shooting expedition, along with his brother Mr William Colquhoun. At the close of the day he re-embarked with a group of his tenants and the spoils of the chase for the return voyage. The wind, although not blowing a gale, had raised an angry surface on the loch. His brother returned alone in advance in a smaller boat and, being an experienced rower, had little difficulty in reaching home. He waited for the arrival of his brother for some time, but in the darkness of the night it was hopeless to start a search. When daylight came the now-empty overturned skiff discovered some distance off, revealing the tragedy which had occurred. The bodies of Sir James and two of his boatmen were found a few days later, not far from the spot where his brother had last seen him.

Henry Bell, the first provost of Helensburgh, was born in 1767 and trained in Glasgow and then in London as a millwright, ship model maker and engineer. He settled in Helensburgh during the late 1790's, having been disappointed by the Admiralty's refusal to investigate his proposals for steam navigation. He diversified and become an hotelier in Dumbarton. He obviously saw the potential for development in the new Burgh of Barony of Helensburgh, and around 1800 built The Baths Hotel, originally some half a mile outside the eastern boundary of the town which at that time ran alongside The Millig Burn.

It is well recorded that Henry Bell was a man of action and often said that, but for him, Helensburgh might have remained green fields and unreclaimed bog. He is described as a restless busy man but he was also a man of noble and kind nature, beloved and trusted by all who had dealings with him – he was forever generous, especially those associated with him in his great work. He was a man of many schemes outside the building of boats and had liberal ideas for what was necessary for the prosperity of the community. Amongst others was the introduction of water, the erection of public markets in the square and the laying of future streets and crescents. But he lacked the means of carrying them out, and the public was apathetic. However, he did what he could in promoting boat building and house building.

Complementary to these sentiments about Henry Bell, there is in Rhu Churchyard a tombstone inscribed:

> To the memory of Captain Robert Bain born May 1788, Died at Fort William December 1827. He was appointed by H. Bell to the command of the Comet steam boat by which vessel a communication was opened up between the Western Islands of Scotland and Glasgow through the Crinan Canal in 1819. He was the first captain who commanded a vessel from sea to sea through the great Caledonian Canal in 1822. This commemoration was erected as a tribute of honour for 16 years faithful service by Henry Bell engineer of Helensburgh

In August 1812 Henry Bell published a program for his steam passage boat between Glasgow, Greenock and Helensburgh, in which he advertised his intention:

> To sail by the power of wind, air and steam and intending that the vessel should leave the Broomielaw on Tuesdays, Thursdays and Saturdays at about mid-day and to leave Greenock Mondays, Wednesdays and Fridays in the morning to suit the tides
>
> The elegance, comfort, safety and speed of this vessel require only to be proved to meet the approbation of the public and the terms are 4 shillings for the best cabin and 3 shillings for the second but beyond these rates, nothing to be paid for the servants.
>
> The advertiser continues his establishment at Helensburgh Baths Hotel and a vessel will be in readiness to convey passengers in comfort from Greenock to Helensburgh"

In those days there was a primitive jetty leading out from the Baths Hotel which in later years could still be seen in outline form. In the early 1800's there seem to have been few industries. There were two or three customer weavers, some coopers and herring curers, a recorded 110 fishermen in the Clyde estuary, a smith and one or two nail makers, besides a considerable number engaged more or less directly in distillation.

In the earlier days of its development the east bay area of Helensburgh was where the wealthy residents resided, but its attraction in comparison with the western side disappeared, in part due to the breakdown of the grid layout, but more to the industrial bias which developed. Not only did the railway begin to divide the upper and lower Helensburgh East, but here also developed the slaughterhouse, the gas works, the steamie and an aerated mineral water works.

A John or Peter Gray had a cooperage at the foot of Maitland Street. There is no doubt he was fully employed, for the herring fishing was productive for several months of the year. There was a small market for fresh fish, but the herring catches had to be cured before being dispatched to Glasgow and other towns in barrels.

At the foot of Maitland Street was a small distillery, but, in common with many districts, there were small illegal stills in Glen Fruin, up the Glennan Burn, at Bannachra and Whistlers Glen. Many were the tales from the older generation of adventures with the Guager and his men, and cunningly laid and executed plans of transit for the amber liquid to neighbouring towns. The smuggler was not the romantic or interesting outlaw of the imagination, but in fact generally a "low, cowardly, surly and lazy type of man. He rarely worked at any honest calling, although might dub himself a mason or shoemaker, but spent most of his time loafing about with red blearied eyes and dirty raynment". The red eyes gave evidence of his confinement for days and nights in some smoky bothy and their inflamed state was caused by continuous "fuddeling", or developing a state of inebriation, when the still did not call for his attendance. "Fuddeling" was then a fine art, and in 1832, when the population of the parish was about two thousand, there were 30 public houses – a traveller from one end of the parish to the other often progressed slowly!

At this time there was a trade in malting and "the Granary, that one hideous object of interest in Clyde Street," was long occupied as a malt barn. An adjacent dock served for shipping the produce, as well as for ferry traffic to Greenock. The trade, however, was never very large and it was killed by competition from other places more favourably situated.

One such location was at Rhu where Whistlers Burn enters the Gareloch. There were two premises of which record is still available, Aldonaig and Broomknowe. There was a significant distillery serviced by a small harbour on the foreshore where the burn enters the

Gareloch. The burn progresses for a mile or more up Whistlers Glen and at this time there were nine cottages,housing the workers in the distillery. The distillery seems to have fallen into disuse about 1830 and subsequently the two properties became residences, one of which is still occupied today.

The name Whistlers Glen came from the practice of signalling the approach of the Excise Officer by whistling. The population of the area were of weak character, and most of the natives instinctively and heartily disliked all physical activity and could shirk it very thoroughly. The men were not afraid of work, they rather enjoyed looking at it and could lie down comfortably beside it. It was told of one that he took two hours to go to his work, two hours to examine it and two hours to return home – he was known as "the express". As a rule the husband had his pride and "prolonged any jobs to the upmost, doing so out of self-respect and to dignify labour".

The boatman – for hiring was an occupation – might as a rule be found in the morning in his favourite public house, during the forenoon sunning himself about the old pier with his hands deep in his pockets and pipe deep in mouth, and when evening drew on and, if no liquor were available, frequenting the smiddy, along with his "compfreers", silently and solemnly blinking at the blaze in the hearth.

And there was still an even lower strata of men, They were a class by themselves and how they supported themselves was an insoluble mystery, but they buttressed the gables of their houses at the pierhead. There were no other ostensible means of livelihood and their visible labour consisted of propping up the walls with their shoulders when they gathered in the evening to talk and smoke.

It may be asked what the other older inhabitants did and how they supported themselves. It is true they were chiefly masons, joiners, fishermen and labourers, but all who possessed houses let lodgings in summer. Annually, about April or May, the row of whitewashed houses fronting the beach broke out in a eruption of tickets bearing the legend "to let furnished". The houses were previously whitewashed internally, as well as externally; the furniture polished and the landlady waiting eagerly the arrival of strangers visiting the hospitable shores.

The Helensburgh Directory for 1834 notes that there were 217 householders in the area, of which 126 offered lodgings, ranging in accommodations from one to 14 rooms.

Everything at the time was subservient to house letting. The grounds were cultivated with patches of cabbage, potatoes and turnips to feed the lodgers. Bargains were driven with lodgers when they did come and when they departed. Much friendly gossip ensued as to the profits made – and then the population seemed to go to sleep for the winter.

The original charter of the Burgh provided for four annual fairs, but these contributed very little, for they were knocked down for five shillings to Robert McNeal. By way of compensation, the council hit on the idea of levying a fee of one shilling annually on each householder for support of the town officer. These annual fairs were kept up for a good many years and a fair business was done selling cattle and hiring servants. They were occasions of festivity for the early inhabitants, with travelling showmen and their human monstrosities, and other attractions – jugglers, acrobats, minstrels, tightrope dancers, gingerbread dealers and candy men. By the 1850's the activities of these fairs had died away, although a thriving annual cattle market continued.

During these times the customer weaver, the itinerant tailor and the travelling shoemaker used to perambulate the country looking for orders and work, to be executed on the spot or elsewhere according to arrangement. These practices died out, leaving no successors. With them went many pleasant associations, and gossip, queer tales and old songs sung by these genial sons of toil around the winter fires of their employers.

There is no doubt that Henry Bell, operating from his Helensburgh base at the Baths Hotel, having commissioned the first steam boat in the world, put Helensburgh at the centre of development of this form of transport. The Comet, built by Wood and Company of Port Glasgow, was the forerunner of many improved developments and a significant role in this was played by Robert Napier.

The Comet 1, which had pioneered commercial steamship navigation, was wrecked of Craignish Point, Argyll, in 1821 and was replaced by Comet 2, built by James Laing in Dumbarton in 1823.

One of the earliest and most catastrophic of steamship disasters took place in the early hours of Friday, 21st October, 1825, when the Comet 2, inward bound from her regular run from Inverness to Glasgow, sank after colliding with the paddle steamer Ayr about 800 yards off Kempock Point, Gourock. Comet 2 sank within three minutes, taking with her around 73 passengers and crew. The final death toll was never ascertained as a check of passengers, either leaving or joining the ship at intermediate ports, was never kept. However, 13 people struggled ashore, including her master Duncan McInnes. The cause of the collision was attributed to the failure of Comet 2 to display any navigation light and the lack of a lookout. Captain McInnes was later charged with culpable homicide and received a three-month jail sentence.

Navigation of the upper Clyde beyond Dumbarton had always been a problem and only navigable by the smallest of vessels. In the 1600's the depth of water in Glasgow was only 14 inches at low tide, and at its highest did not exceed three feet. In the mid 1600's Glasgow town council negotiated with Dumbarton for the latter to become their port. This was turned down by the Dumbarton Council, on the grounds that the presence of too many mariners would raise the cost of food to the inhabitants.

The Glasgow council negotiated a lease of lands to build new Port Glasgow in the late 1600's, but, because of lack of progress on this and its practical application, they lost interest and the Glasgow council exercised its mind of making the Clyde navigable. They attempted unsuccessfully to remove the formidable sandbank at Dumbuck, By 1770 they had obtained an Act of Parliament authorising the deepening of the Clyde channel to at least seven feet in low water. A John Golborne of Chester got the contract to deepen the Dumbuck ford to at least six feet. This increased itself to 14 feet as a consequence of the increasing scour of the river over subsequent years.

In 1840 an additional Act was passed by Parliament authorising the deepening of the river throughout to at least 17 feet at neap tides, and laying down lines for future widening. The greatest natural obstacle proved to be a rock at Elderslie which had been discovered by the grounding of a ship in 1854. It extended across the river for nearly 1000 feet, and it cost £70,000 to cut through this rock to a depth of 20 feet below low water. Only in about 1900 was the last of the rock removed. In 1800 the high tide in Glasgow was three hours later than at Port Glasgow, but following the widening and deepening of the river, it was reduced to about only one hour later

Robert Napier was born in Dumbarton in 1789 and educated at the grammar school there. In his early years, he developed a taste for architectural and mechanical drawing and designing. During an apprenticeship to the Millrowten Smith business he distinguished himself on ornamental designs and workmanship. At the close of his apprenticeship he went with a few pounds in his pocket to Edinburgh, to find his way in the world.

At an early age we find him promoted to a high position in the employment of Robert Stevenson, Engineers, where his powers found wider exercise. In 1815, when but 24 years of age, he started a business on his own account in Glasgow. From the occupation of a modest workshop in the Greyfriars Wynd, he gradually advanced to proprietorship of a large business. When the application of steam to ships became established, he devoted his skill to the construction of the machinery for them.

As a successor to the Comet, one of the first vessels to be developed was The Helensburgh of 125 tons, built by Robert Napier and propelled by a 52 horsepower engine.

Following this development, work rapidly flowed in for other vessels plying to Belfast and Liverpool. From that time his name became widely known and work poured in from all corners of the world. The first steamers were built of wood, but he introduced iron which gradually superseded the wooden hulls. The governments of this and other countries gave him large orders for warships and transport vessels, and his great works at Lancefield and Govan were the scene of a busy industry for many years. Honours and decorations were showered upon him in recognition of his services to international communications and trade. But, with all the wealth and honours he attained, he retained an inauspicious life of simple manners. When he retired from active duty to the beautiful retreat he had built at West Shandon, it gave him a great deal of pleasure to show off his art gallery with its significant collection of paintings and antiques. But there was one article he probably set more store by and more fondly exhibited – his mother's spinning wheel.

Shortly after his death in 1876, his magnificent collection was sold in London and realised £49,743. West Shandon House passed into the hands of a hydropathic company. It was enlarged and subsequently became one of the most popular health resorts in Scotland, occupying a charming and sheltered situation, with the grounds beautifully laid out, and the view from the windows unrivalled. It was frequented by visitors from all parts of the world.

In the late 1700's a feuing plan of Helensburgh was commissioned from Charles Ross of Greenlaw, surveyor to the Luss estates, yet it was not until 1803 that the grid layout concept materialised in a survey of the town carried out by Peter Fleming of Glasgow. It involved a grid system of streets, 60 feet wide, with feus of minimum size, the whole built around the concept of a harbour on the shoreline, with a straight street leading up the hillside in what is currently Colquhoun Street. One street back from the shoreline was Colquhoun Square and then the road continued right up the hillside so that the vista from the top looked straight down and out to the harbour. This was the original concept, many aspects of which have been incorporated with integrity.

In 1845 a survey of Helensburgh streets recorded many shortcomings, especially in the matter of footpaths. Clyde Street, as far as Adelaide Street, had no footpaths on the north side as all the properties encroached upon the street. The lower end of Maitland Street was for the most part under rubbish and nettles, and John Street and Glenfinlas Street were not yet properly formed. Water ran across Princes Street, and King Street was impassable, from the Glennan Burn to Sinclair Street. The path at the lower end of James Street at the Tabernacle required dressing and levelling. Colquhoun Square was in very bad order, with no footpath around it, and more of a nuisance than an ornament. Dunghills created a nuisance in several places, and about half of Adelaide Street had been fenced in by the residents and planted with trees.

The original plan of the town included a harbour, the cost of which was to be met by a government grant of £1,500, if an equal amount could be raised by the town. The town, however, fell short of the target by £400, and in 1810 it was recorded that a small harbour for coasting vessels was being constructed with a stone dyke. It was built in 1816, lengthened by some 30 yards in 1822 and taken over by the council in 1834. This put an end to the proposal to develop a proper harbour with two piers and an entrance into a deeper water basin. One theory of the day suggests that it was being built in the wrong place, as a rock on the eastern side of the pier interfered with navigation so much that steamers often had to land their passengers at Rosneath.

In 1837 the Colquhoun proprietors feued to the council the ground to the east of the granary which was to be kept clear for pier improvements. This put paid to the market which the Provost wished to erect on that ground. Nothing very much was done, for it was said in 1854 that there was an apology for a harbour. Although it was re-constructed in 1859 for £3,775, it was very clear that the state of the pier was a sore point in Helensburgh for most of the century.

It is an interesting social commentary to identify the activities within Greenock as a leading town in the region during the early

1800's, the period during which the town was beginning to be established as a residential area.

Greenock had become the leading town and market within the West of Scotland area, in part through its trade via the river to foreign parts, but as much to the foresightedness of the same Shaw family who had sold the lands on which Helensburgh is situated to the Colquhouns in 1756.

Sir John Shaw of Ardgowen, as Baron of the Barony of Greenock, granted a new charter in 1751 which gave the feuers and sub-feuers and burgesses authorisation to meet and elect magistrates, councillors and managers for the formation of a town council. This delegation of power paid great dividends, and it is recorded that the charter he granted in 1751 may be justly regarded as the foundation stone of the prosperity of Greenock. The privilege which it bestowed gave to its inhabitants an interest in its welfare and security and control over the development of the economy. At the present time the Shaw family is still in possession of Ardgowen, under the name of Shaw Stewart.

The leading citizen of Greenock during this period was James Watt, the celebrated improver of the steam engine, who was born in Greenock in 1736. He was involved in the development of the condenser for steam engines and created the technology with which the Comet could be built, assisting significantly in the development of the Helensburgh community.

James Watt had one of the most illustrious careers in engineering, in particular through the development of steam engines which began to drive the economic power of the world. The little-known effect was that the the French Academy of Sciences recorded for Mr Watt the honour of being the first to discover the composition of water. They stated that in the month of April, 1783, experiments with condensation and steam engines had led Watt to conclude that water was a compound of only two gasses, oxygen and hydrogen, and that this was the first proof of the phenomenon.

Proof of the economic development of Greenock can be drawn in part from the population statistics. In 1755 there were about 3,800 of a population. By 1800 it had risen to 17,400, and by 1831 to 27,500.

Indicative of the ingenuity in pursing economic development was the scheme drawn up in 1824 to provide Greenock with water for consumption and power. On the high ground between two and three miles above Greenock were a large number of small rivers, uniting with other streams and falling to the sea. It was proposed to form an embankment to create a large reservoir at the source of this water, and then to conduct it round the hill by open aqueduct. The water would be passed down two branches, one descending on the western, the other on the eastern extremity of the town, each containing falls of different levels of power to suit the different manufacturers. The proposed reservoir would cover 200 acres and contain 200 million cubic feet of water. The length of the aqueduct and related channels would be six and a half miles.

This scheme was brought to fruition by 1825 and a joint stock company with a capital of £31,000 Scottish was incorporated by an Act of Parliament.

The descent of water down the channels was cleverly designed. There were 19 falls of different degrees of power on the eastern line and 13 in the western. The extent of the falls had been designed for various purposes. The quantity of water going down each of the two falls was sufficient to give power for impelling machinery equal to that of 54 horses. Taking the whole scheme of falls on two watercourses, the water power was equal to 1,782 horses. This achievement by the Shaw Water Company, directed by Mr Robert Tom, civil engineer and proprietor of Rothesay cotton works, a man of fertile invention and extraordinary mechanical genius, was the source and provider of the impetus for Greenock's position in the economic development of the region.

Each fall, and the provision of power generated, was carefully calculated and industry developed as an integral part of the design. For example, fall number one on the eastern end was of 26 feet, or 47 horse power, and was used by Tasker Young and Company to power a sugar house; fall two, a flour and corn mill; fall three, a flour mill, fall four, a wool factory; fall five, an iron foundry; fall six, a chemical works; fall seven, a rice mill and fall 10, a paper mill,.

This development was one of the most imaginative and significant in the world and provided the impetus that made Greenock such a wealthy town, which even today can by seen by the style of its houses and public buildings. The branches of manufacturing which benefited from this unique system were ship and boat building, iron founding and forging, sugar refining, rope spinning, sail cloth manufacturing, sail making, paper making, tanning, currying of leather, earthenware manufacture, wool and cloth and yarn making, coopers and joiners work, cabinet making, chipping of log wood, flour and oatmeal manufacturing, brewing and distilling. A glass furnace cone and relative buildings were at one time occupied as a bottle works and crystal factory.

With the knowledge that Scotland, and in particular the Clyde valley, had become engineers to the world, it is interesting to note from the Second Statistical Account that in 1840 there were three iron foundries and forges, employing 1,000 people. In these were made all sorts of cast iron and machinery, steam boilers and engines. One company alone furnished machinery for more than 40 steamers of the largest class and a considerable number of English-built steamers had been sent to Greenock to receive their machinery.

The strongest transport links were across the Clyde with Port Glasgow and Greenock, and similarly Rosneath had communications chiefly by water, as there were no turnpike roads in that parish. On Loch Lomond regular steamers ran from May to the end of October, for the roads did not permit the use of heavy coaches.

For much of the 1800's there were frequent ferries across the Clyde at about a dozen points, ranging from Dalmuir to Kilcreggan, as well as several across the Gareloch and Loch Long. By the middle of the 1800's many piers had been built for steamers on Garelochside.

Dumbarton and Helensburgh piers were enlarged and at one time three steamship companies were running competitive services linking Arrochar, Garelochhead, Kilcreggan, Cove, Helensburgh and Dumbarton, Bowling and Old Kilpartick and Glasgow with places across the Clyde. Piers were built at all these points but very few remain.

An example of the paddle steamers emerging in the late 1800's, many of which were good for at least 15 knots, was the Lucy Ashton. She left Garelochhead promptly at 7 am and called at Mambeg, Rahane ferry, Shandon, Barremman (the former name of Clynder), Rosneath, and Rhu, for Helensburgh and Craigendoran, arriving in time for the businessmen to catch the Glasgow train. She made the return voyage at noon, and left Garelochhead again at 2 pm for ladies to do their shopping in Helensburgh. These wives picked up their spouses from the 4 o'clock train from Glasgow and they all arrived at Garelochhead about 6 pm.

When, however, the railway companies bought out the steamship companies and built Craigendoran pier in 1883, the whole of the Clyde steamer traffic concentrated there. Loch Lomond had competitive steamer services, whilst the Leven was a navigable waterway until the 1860's.

The Forth and Clyde Canal, which was completed in 1790, offered a harbour and basin at Bowling where the trans-shipment of goods from the larger seagoing vessels to canal boats was conducted. The canal was immensely important in the early 1800's.

The earliest railway in Scotland, apart from the light railway from Kilmarnock to Troon, was the Monkland and Kirkintilloch, which started in 1826 with horse drawn wagons. These were converted to locomotives in 1831, the whole being designed for the transport of coal from the Lanarkshire field to the Forth and Clyde Canal. The canals declined fairly early as passenger carriers, though popular excursions continued to run between 1890 and 1939. Transport of goods was very important and increased in volume until 1868. The canal had been acquired by the Caledonian Railway Company in 1867 and there was a steady decrease in trade as rail transport took over.

By 1830 the change from predominantly rural to industrial ways had developed significantly. At the time of the census in 1841, Dumbarton, Kirkintilloch and Cumbernauld were substantial towns, and, of the villages, only Old Kilpatrick and Renton were of any size, the latter being the first to show growth that was entirely dependant on industry. There were 18 villages whose population was over 1,000. These were mainly in the Vale of Leven and the Kilpatricks and they straggled along near the mills and streams, having no connections with the old centres grouped round a church or a big house. The large-scale packing of tenements and factories in towns did not occur until the late 1800's. Whilst the old towns were still growing, the truly phenomenal growth was in the new Clydebank.

The change-over to town life brought many problems, especially of health, sanitation and water supply. The cholera epidemic in Dumbarton in 1832 gave the first shock to the public conscience. The local board of health was set up when it was realised that the two doctors for Dumbarton, one beside the churchyard the other by the slaughterhouse, both had queues from early morning in the summer time. They were, to say the least, inadequate.

The middle 1800's was a period of substantial railway development and the railway into Helensburgh was constructed about 1857.

It was proposed, following the success of railway enterprises in England, to build a railway from Glasgow to Greenock, via Paisley and Port Glasgow. The reason for doing this was hotly disputed by the shipping fraternity. In a very short time the project was accepted. A company was set up, the requisite number of shares was subscribed and an Act of Parliament was applied for and obtained in 1837. The work made rapid progress and was to be completed in about 1840. The high price of the shares, when compared to stock of a similar kind, indicated the confidence which the shareholders and the public held.

The railway company were no doubt conscious that by removing people from Glasgow to Greenock, a distance of 22 miles, they were enabling the public to use steamers and travel to more distant parts in one easy process, under their total control.

The extensive construction of the railway, including stations, engines, and carriages, was calculated £22,000 Scots per mile. After making allowance for keeping the railway in repair, the directors anticipated a clear dividend of 12 percent of the shareholders' money. The railway companies, who brought the track down the north side of the Clyde to Helensburgh, had ambitions to create a pier head for steamer sailings.

Before the 1840's each town in Britain kept its own time, to make maximum use of daylight. This would have caused significant problems in timetabling rail services, so the Government passed an Act of Parliament in 1840 enforcing London time on the entire British Isles. Plymouth and Exeter temporarily held out against the imposition Greenwich Standard Time but it was not long before this was adopted nationally, probably to the discomfort of the more northern locations, such as Helensburgh and its surrounding area.

Chapter 10   AD 1850 – 1900

Railway Development –Helensburgh Water Supply –Development of the Town – Golf Club – Sporting facilities – Early Roads – Distillery – Gas Works – Harbour – Cemetery – Cairndhu Inn – Ardencaple Castle

The development of railways moved apace in the period around 1850 when the country was in the grip of railway mania. It was about that time that the railway line from Glasgow to Kirkintilloch and Lennoxtown was built. Shortly afterwards the Helensburgh link with Dalreoch was built privately. It was later taken over by the North British Railway Company, and Glasgow was connected to Bowling at the same time.

This heralded a race to the coast, the speed of which has never been equalled since. In 1890 11 trains interconnecting with 13 boats were run for passengers leaving Glasgow in the half hour after 4 pm. On Saturdays the same thing happened two hours earlier, and at 9.30 am every day the same procedure held good in reverse. The Caledonian Railway Company ran a service on the southside, via Gourock to Kilcreggan and Cove, taking 47 and 55 minutes respectively. The North British Railway Company on the Dunbartonshire side took 55 and 65 minutes.

Roads were very primitive at the beginning of the modern period and in 1810 there were only 90 miles of turnpike in the shire, mainly east of the Leven, but by 1864 there were 131 miles. The Leven was bridged at Dumbarton in 1865, at Bonhill in 1836 and at Balloch in 1841, so that the area west of the Leven was no longer isolated. Coaches, as well as carriers, plied daily between Dumbarton and Glasgow.

The development of railways transformed the area. One early line was the Bowling – Balloch line of the Caledonian and Dumbarton Railway, completed in 1850. The line extended as far as Balloch pier.

Direct link with Glasgow became possible in 1858 when that line was joined with the Glasgow, Dumbarton and Helensburgh line. By 1870 Balloch was connected by rail to Stirling, but this closed to passenger traffic in the late 1930's and to goods in 1957.

In 1857 the Glasgow, Dumbarton and Helensburgh railway, which was by then a branch of the North British system, was opened. It gave the first real impetus to progress and enhancement in the value of property. There is no doubt that the railway company and its promoters justified the expense of this line with the thought that they could develop ferry terminals at Helensburgh to meet up with the steamboats then proliferating along the lochs.

When the railway first came into Helensburgh, it stopped at the Grant Street station. Even today, there is an iron footbridge over the line at this point which was part of the original station. For a number of years there remained a strong lobby for the railway line to be extended along the East Bay and on to the pier, but an equally large body of opinion, led by William Kidston, succeeded in defeating the provision. In 1900 it was reported that the community had since continuously mourned the loss of the station on the sea and 3,000 householders had petitioned the railway company to revive the matter. Instead of improving the existing station they should construct a new one at the pier. The proposal subsequently drifted away and the fine facilities at Craigendoran were built on the outskirts of the town, which became the leading centre for train/boat traffic until the pier closed down about 1972.

The station moved in two stages to its present position adjacent to the town buildings on the corner of Sinclair Street and Princes Street. The present building was constructed in 1899. In the year 2001 this station was again modified, the platforms being re-roofed, the part of the property adjacent to the town offices converted into offices and the ticket office moved further along the platform.

The question of a water supply to the town was debated on a protracted basis from the beginning of the 1800's when the supply of the inhabitants was drawn from shallow wells and one or two natural springs. They were inadequate and many of the wells were collecting surface water of doubtful purity. These had been dug by the old proprietors who clung tenaciously to the pump handle and rebelled against any water scheme, ridiculed it, condemned it and drew graphic pictures of the town plunged into debt.

In the early 1800's Henry Bell's fertile and farseeing mind contemplated introducing a water supply to the young community from Glen Fruin. A survey was made and plans prepared showing an artificial lake on the bed of the stream on the Farm of Kilbride, but there was little public interest and no money to carry out the scheme, and it consequently lapsed.

From 1820 to 1860 the matter was occasionally talked about but no action was taken, so slowly did the wheels of government move. Shortly after this Dr Robert Hendry, then a Bailie, raised the question of promoting a scheme for the construction of a reservoir in the upper reaches of the Glennan Burn and leading the storage into street wells throughout the town. This was abandoned when it was found that the reliability of supply was suspect.

Undeterred by former failures, the matter was again raised in 1866 by Provost Breingen, who was to the fore in many public improvements. The population had risen from 3,000 in 1851 to 5,000 by 1861, and was still rapidly increasing, but the lack of a water supply was inhibiting the growth. Notwithstanding objections from a strong minority, a scheme was adopted by the ratepayers, and in March 1868 the Mainhills reservoir and filter works were formally opened amid general rejoicing. The ceremony was performed by Mrs Breingen at the Old Filter House at the top of Sinclair Street, where she opened the water taps. The building is on the right hand side at the top of Sinclair Street and is now a house, having been converted in the late 1970's. A door onto Sinclair Street indicates where this property was, surrounded now by Walker's Rest Park, donated by the Colquhouns to the town as a leisure area on the edge of the countryside.

From the middle of the 1800's anxiety about public health grew and the matter of a public hospital was much discussed. Temporary provision for patients with infectious diseases had been obtained by leasing a disused malt barn in Maitland Street. The accommodation was very limited and the building totally unsuitable.

Fortunately, a benevolent lady, Miss Anne Alexander, of Lomond Cottage, was concerned and in her will bequeathed the residue of her estate to aid in the erection of a hospital. In conjunction with the local authority, the hospital now standing at the end of East King Street was completed in 1875. In the initial periods the lower floor was devoted to accident cases and general sickness, the upper floor to infectious diseases. The management of the lower wards was conferred on a committee who undertook to meet its operating expenses.

A Mr John Stewart was elected provost in 1877 and was responsible for many improvements in the town during his period in office. First was the erection of suitable municipal buildings, adjacent to the railway station. He did much to improve the sanitary condition of the foreshore and drainage of the town. He reclaimed the east bay from the encroachment of the sea and laid it out as an esplanade, adding a very attractive resort for the Eastenders . His successor, Provost Bryson (1884 – 1890), continued the good work and fresh improvements were carried out at the west esplanade. It had formerly extended from the pier to the west burn and was extended to the boundary of the town.

He also secured the handsome building still used as a post office in Princess Street and was responsible for the erection of the Victoria Halls, an imposing and commodious building in Sinclair Street, paid for by private subscription. After completion it was handed over to the Burgh Commission in trust for the public. He also succeeded in successfully concluding the difficult negotiations with the promoters of the West Highland Railway Line.

During the second half of the 1800's life went at a slower pace. Even the jokes were handed down from father to son as heirlooms.

They were so rare that they became household treasures and were venerated because of their antiquity. Perhaps this is an area where nothing has changed today!.

Twice a year a fair was held where gingerbread, nuts and sweetmeat stalls abounded, and itinerant acrobats exhibited their feats. Occasionally a travelling circus or menagerie visited. In winter there were lectures on instructive subjects such as savings banks, starch manufacturing, coal or chemistry, the last always being the most popular because of the dazzling blue and yellow lights produced and horrible smells produced.

The only outdoor amusements were coits or shinty matches on the lands at the seafront, and shooting matches for a sheep on New Year's Day. Football, bowls, cricket, lawn tennis, golf and croquet had yet to come to the area.

The want of a recreation ground for both young and old was for a long time deplored, because other places had ample provision, even communities of much less importance in size or population or natural advantages. The much-needed facilities were subsequently provided, thanks to the late Sir James Colquhoun, who during the 1870's gave land at nominal rates for public facilities. Amongst these he gave two acres of land adjoining Sinclair Street for a bowling green which was laid out at considerable expense in three separate greens. There were also tennis grounds in the West End of the town, in a field belonging to ex-Provost Breingan, well laid out and provided with ample shelter and every convenience. About 1860 Sir James Colquhoun and other gentlemen granted a charter to the magistrates for a number of acres at the west of town, on Rhu Road Higher, for the creation of a cricket and quoits ground. This remains as green belt, still used by the Cricket and Rugby Club. All these activities fell away a little after golf was brought to the town. The founding of Helensburgh Golf Club on Monday, August 14th, 1893, was not before time and after several abortive attempts. As a leading article in *The Helensburgh and Gareloch Times* the previous week had noted:

There are few towns now of any importance that cannot boast a golf course. The want of such a place of recreation has been felt to be of such hindrance to the prosperity of the town.

At one time or another there have been golf courses at Shandon, Garelochhead, Tarbet, Kilcreggan and Finart. Of those which remain, Dumbarton was formed in 1888 and Cardross in 1895. An advertisement in the *Helensburgh and Gareloch Times* of August 9th, 1893, convened a meeting for the consideration of the proposed golf club. We can see from adjacent advertisements that there was stiff competition to attract the population. At the same time there is billed a visit of the Bostocks Grand Star Menagerie, whose exhibits included the untameable lion 'Wallace', the wonderful performing musical elephant who was to be introduced by General Mite Tiny, the smallest trainer in the world. Also entertaining at the same time was Miss Bessy Arthur, "the greatest vocalist and comic entertainer that Scotland has yet produced". In spite of these competing attractions the meeting was well attended and the golf club formally formed, with Sir James Colquhoun honorary president and Alexander Breingan as first captain. Included in the committee was one A.B. Law who, as Andrew Bonner Law, became Prime Minister in 1923.

Within 24 days of the meeting, the membership had reached 120, and 49 had put up debentures of £5 each which funded the original course development. Fifty-four days after the first meeting some enthusiasts were reported to have played the first course, and the maximum membership had almost been reached.

The stumbling block for the formation of the golf club had until this time been the Colquhoun Trustees who would not sanction the terms of the agreement with the tenant of Kirkmichael Farm. The promoters of the club had identified land at the farm as the best they could get close to the town, and had identified 40 acres of the high park, east and west of the old Luss road, at an annual rent of 35 shillings per acre, the farmer retaining the whole grazing. The

Colquhoun Trustees eventually agreed to the leasing of the land and offered the club a new tenure lease in 1897, at a rent of 30 shillings per acre, with the club retaining the grazing rights.

The secretary of the club, William Lunan, had obtained a plan of a corrugated iron club house which could be erected for less than £200 and this was acquired and situated to the west of the old Luss Road, somewhere in the region of the fairway of the current eighteenth hole. The course was of a nine-hole layout, designed by Old Tom Morris who had won four Open Championships.

Old Tom had two strict rules on course maintenance. The first was "mair saun" (more sand) which he claimed was the basis of good turf; the second "nae Sunday play – the course needs a rest even if the Gowfere don't". This latter was observed for more that 30 years.

Further developments took place when the tin hut clubhouse was relocated in 1900 close to the West Highland railway line in Abercromby Street for reasons of easier access. The demand for golf facilities increased rapidly and the course was extended to 18 holes by 1905. By 1908 the Helensburgh committee had resolved to build a new clubhouse on the site of the present clubhouse. The old core of the present clubhouse building was built at a cost of around £2,700, funded by debentures issued to members, the last of which was repaid in about 1950. The clubhouse was opened in 1909 by the Duke of Argyll.

For winter recreation a stretch of ground about four acres in extent was given by the late Sir James Colquhoun on the moor above the town and a skating pond developed. To meet the aspirations of the older men a curling pond was provided at the east end of the town, in Havelock Street.

In the 1700's the roads in the area, more accurately described as tracks, were formed principally for foot or horseback travel. Perhaps the best known was the Old Luss Road, developed by the Duke of Argyll, to link him from the Drumfork Ferry over the hills on his way to Inverary. At the time of writing, the track can still be walked. It winds up the eastern boundary of the town, through the golf course and over the hill into Glen Fruin, where it divides, one road going down into Glen Fruin and onto Faslane Bay, the other winding down to Loch Lomond side at Arden or onward to Luss. A small whitewashed building stands where this division takes place. Currently a residence, it is known as Crosskeys, harking back to its previous incarnation as a drovers' inn.

The road coming through Glen Fruin from Portincaple, Whistlefield and Faslane Bay divides towards the eastern end. It continues left to Crosskeys and branches right to join Old Luss Road and Drumfork Ferry. It was at this point that there was a mill and a one-room school to accommodate the significant population of the glen in former days.

The Highlandman's Way is often used to describe many of the paths and routes used today. The original Highlandman's Way, before modern roads were built, was the route from Arrochar to Dumbarton which passed along the hilltop ridges, by-passing the tolls houses along the route. This passed along the hills behind Helensburgh and Cardross, before dipping down to Dumbarton. Routes from Portincaple and Rhu came up the hillsides to join the main track.

There is also a track still used for social walking. In former times it was the drove road joining Garelochside and Glen Fruin. When Rhu church was the only place of worship in the parish, this road was the Sabbath day's journey of the inhabitants of Glen Fruin who numbered some 300 in 1700, drawn by the relatively fertile land and protection afforded by the surrounding hills from the winds and enemies coming up the Clyde.

As Helensburgh evolved, the main access inland from the shoreline was up what is now known as Sinclair Street, named after The Sutherland family of Sinclair, into which the Colquhoun family married. In early days it was known as New Luss Road, in its early days reaching as far up the hill as the bowling club where it turned to the right and traversed the hillside behind Chapleacre and joined up with the Old Luss Road, the only passage over the hill in these early days.

Before the coming of the railway in the 1850's the growth of the burgh was not spectacular, but Helensburgh was a well-ordered little place, "well supplied with shops of every description". Houses first sprung up along Clyde Street between the Glennan Burn, where the first house was Augusta Lodge, still there today. It was the home of Lady Augusta Claverling and had a garden leading down towards the shore.

In the eastern end of the town, by 1840 houses reached along Clyde Street as far as MacDonald Street, and behind there were rows of neat white cottages, each with its garden. Princes Street then hardly extended further east than Maitland Street, and there was not much of King Street or Argyll Street beyond Suffolk Street to the west and Grant Street to the east.

The town well was still in use on the north side of King Street midway between Sinclair and George Streets, and the western boundary was known simply as Ardencaple March. The east end of the town was still dominated by the Baths Hotel, the only other hotel being the Tontine Inn, a posting house at the quay head owned by a Robert Glen. It had hot and cold water, baths and a stagecoach service every morning to meet the steamer at Luss.

The post office was in Clyde Street, and a mail gig left there every evening. There was also an afternoon foot post, in addition to the local mail runner, John Dingwall.

At the corner of Clyde and Maitland Streets was the distillery founded by Messrs A and J Stein, who had Scotland's largest distillery at that time in Paisley, known as the Saucel distillery. The Helensburgh distillery could produce 400 gallons a week of the finest malt whisky. Its lease was advertised thus in 1838:

The water is the best quality for making fine malt whisky being collected over nearly 3 acres of moss in a long dam.

With reference to this latter claim, it is only speculation to assume that because of the closeness of the Millig Burn that the water was taken from this and the moss referred to was possibly the mill lade in what is now Hermitage Park.

Helensburgh was then a well-doctored town, with at least five doctors, some with the highest qualifications, the first, Doctor Duncan, having set up practice as far back as 1808. The first provident or savings bank was started about 1827 in Clyde Street, with Peter McCallum, draper, as manager.

In 1843 a gas works was built on the outskirts of the town just to east of Maitland Street. Coal was shipped from the Lanarkshire coal fields. The boats were beached and the coal moved into the gas works by horse and cart. Gas was first used for lighting the town in 1846 and slowly improved throughout the century, despite of the town council's rather meagre provision of lamps. As late as 1899 a petition was organised to prevent an extension of the gas works towards the west end of the town. But the works were extended and became a very substantial facility, where, at the time of writing, the gas holder stands. Hearsay suggests that from this gas works a pipeline serviced Rhu and the Shandon lochside. Just below the Barbour Cemetery on the Rosneath peninsular there was also a gas works, the remnants of which can still be seen. It supplied the Kilcreggan, Cove, Rosneath area with a pipeline to the big houses along the shoreline.

The first attempt to bring the railway to Helensburgh proved abortive. In 1846 the promoters of the Caledonian and Dunbartonshire Railway Company made an agreement with the council to take the railway to a point between Colqhoun Street and Sinclair Street, west of the present terminus, and to put down rails from there across Princes Street to the quay. To finance this the company were to make a loan of £3,000, and the council increasing the pier dues.

The next year the company wanted to make various deviations to the original line between Camis Eskan Gate and Helensburgh which would have seriously effected the amenity of the east end of the town where most of the feus existed for private houses and summer quarters. It would have shut off certain streets and blocked access to the parish church at the foot of Sinclair Street. The council, against the judgment of Provost Richard Kidston, obstinately tried to force the railway company to meet its obligations when it secured a Railway Bill in Parliament. They finally admitted defeat in the House of Lords in 1854 and Helensburgh was still without a railway. Three years later, however, it arrived, with a terminus initially in Grant Street which later moved to its final and current position adjacent to the civic buildings just to the east of Sinclair Street. The railway to the pier never materialised.

As the century wore on a section of the townspeople still yearned for a new station on the waterfront, rather than an extension to the existing pier. This was carried out about 1879, at a cost of £11,000 Scots, to accommodate the North British steamboats. Two years later this company planned to build a pier at Craigendoran, one mile east of the town. The move was bitterly opposed by the Helensburgh Harbour Trust and fell through for the time being. However, in 1877 the same company decided to bring the railway to a terminus on Helensburgh seafront, but this proposal split the town, and, thanks to the opposition organised by William Kidston, it was thrown out. The harbour itself was deepened in 1880, as a result of the complaints of captains that they had been touching sand for the past 30 years. In 1882 the North British Railway Company,k thwarted by the town of Helensburgh, finally built their pier at Craigendoran and this became the centre of train/steamer interface for the Clyde estuary, which continued until its discontinuation in the 1970's.

In 1846 a Police Act was obtained under which the affairs of the town could be managed. The governing officials were increased in number and the powers conferred on them expanded to enable them to improve order. The streets were formerly badly kept, ill-drained and unlit. After nearly 20 years' effort on behalf of the corporation everything was in good condition, although not so well lit as it ought to have been, but better than most country towns.

One great drawback to the prosperity of the town for many years was the want of a good harbour. The original town plan included a harbour enclosed by two piers and £1,500 was made available by the government towards its formation, on condition that an equal amount was raised locally. The sum on the subscription list, though it reached £1,100, fell short of the target and the matter was allowed to drop. The pier, originally a stone dyke for landing and embarking passengers from steamers and small boats, was lengthened and increased by degrees. It was under the management of a committee of subscribers till 1834, when a piece of ground to the east of the pier was purchased by the town council from Mr Henry Taylor to turn it into a bazaar or market place.

This plan was superseded by Sir James Colquhoun making a grant to the council of all the vacant ground eastward to the granary, on condition that the ground be kept clear for improvements to the pier and for accommodation of passengers. As the original subscribers to the pier had no right of property they transferred their management to the town council, in hope of an improved and enlarged pier and harbour being erected. This never happened; but a tolerable pier now supersedes the old stone dyke. The lack of a harbour was, however, less likely to be felt since direct railway communications with Glasgow had opened up.

Contemporary records are probably the most reliable ones to quote in illustrating the state of development, and in 1865 Battrum published his second edition 'Guide to Helensburgh'. Battrum was located in Helensburgh, opposite the railway station, and the business was subsequently taken over by MacNeur and Bryden which continued with its regular updates of the guides to the area until the 1980's. These can be deemed a reliable source of information about the area.

Battrum reported that since the opening of the railway in 1857 the great impulse to building in the neighbourhood and the size of the place had almost doubled, as well as the value of property. The population in 1851 was 2,895 and had risen ten years later to 4,769. During the early 1860's the progress of building had very much decreased, notwithstanding a continual demand for houses. Various causes had contributed to this but chiefly amongst them were the want of regular water supply and the limited number of walks and drives in the neighbourhood available to invalids.

The guide described the general plan of Helensburgh as a good one and:

if fully carried out cannot fail to render it, as far as available means are concerned, both an attractive and a healthy place of residence. It is built on ground rising with easy access from the sea and for fully a mile back this gradual elevation continues. It possesses therefore great facilities for thorough drainage and for the maintenance for every necessary sanitary regulation. The town is laid off in rectangle squares and each of these contains about two acres of ground.

There is an abundance of wide open streets securing a larger space of breathing ground than is found in most modern towns and there is little danger of over cramming the buildings for, except in the two principal streets, Clyde and Princes Street, the number of houses on each acre is restricted to at the most four and in many cases to two. The houses except in these two streets are chiefly in the cottage style offering every variety of design and size of construction, although of late years taste has run more in erection of mansions of a larger and handsome appearance, equal if not superior, in many cases to the best country seats. To each house is attached a considerable piece of garden ground which are generally tastefully laid off in flowers and shrubbery. The prevailing errors of landscape design which seems to rule at Scotch watering places has done something to mar the beauty and destroy the attractiveness of Helensburgh as a popular resort. The idea has always been to confirm it in appearance as much as possible to a commercial town which it will never be and all bits of attractive scenery have been carefully removed; the streets have been levelled with most judicious care; the streams bridged over and covered out of sight and the square and park utterly divested of any ornament whatsoever.

A well macadamised road is no doubt a great boom – indeed so is plenty of road way whether ill or well kept, but the great fact so thoroughly kept in few continental watering places that the prosperity of the place depends more on its attractiveness than its pure useful features. The idea and practice has been – route the visitor or inhabitor out of every cover; keep him to acres of bare street; give him no shelter, no pleasant wooded haunt: let the noonday sun bask and beat on him and provide him with a park instead of a shade; let there be no cooling fountain refreshing to the sense anywhere an if overpower by heat and dust and anxious longing for a plunge in the clear and inviting waters of the bay the visitor should seek this solace and keep him back from denying him every facility for such a pleasure.

Again in 1865 Battrum reports that of late years the rapidly increasing population had effected a change in the character of the property in the front street:

Most of the old building have been taken down and replaced by handsome modern erections fitted up for shops. Of these there are almost every variety some of them equal to those in the first towns in the kingdom and in which an abundance supply of every article essential to comfort and luxury can be procured. There are no buildings of any antiquity to interest the visitors. The almost only public buildings are the churches and banks.

Battrum in his own inimitable contemporary style has described what is perhaps the resident's view of the town in the early 1860's, but what it does indicate is that the town had embarked on a process of becoming a residential rather than an industrial or commercial town and that shops were being built to service all the needs of the increasingly affluent, residential population that was developing up the hillside.

To show how quickly the town began to grow about that time, we can refer to the first directory of Helensburgh which was 'Fowlers Directory', published in 1834, which records premises by premises the occupational use of each establishment. Perhaps a more prominent mention in that directory was that James Breinagan, later a Provost of the town, had premises on East Clyde Street where he traded as a grocer, wine and spirit merchant, postmaster and Procurator Fiscal.

In 1830, again on East Clyde Street, a reading or news room was opened which had amongst its periodicals, two London papers daily. The subscription was one guinea per annum, or ten shillings and six pence for the sea bathing season.

The directory also recorded the advertisement of carrier services, for wagons going to Dumbarton and Glasgow, departing on a Tuesday and arriving in Glasgow on a Wednesday, and to Garelochhead twice weekly. So land-based transport was beginning to evolve.

It is also interesting to note from the Directory that the population of Helensburgh in 1834 had risen to 1,200, of which 69 people were qualified to vote – "all those of a legal age who have a feu or lease on a property of 100 years or more".

Battrum reported in his Town Guide that of late years the rapidly increasing population had effected a change in the character of the property in the front street – most of the old building having been taken down and replaced by handsome modern erections fitted out for shops:

Of these there were almost every variety, some of the equal to those in the first towns in the Kingdom, and of which an abundant supply of every article essentially counted as a luxury can by procured. By 1867 it was recorded that, Inter Alia, there were 3 dentists, 2 watch and clock makers, 4 doctors, 4 midwives, 2 photographers, 2 umbrella makers and 2 writers.

A sure sign that prosperity had arrived, came with the introduction of the banks. The first was a savings bank promoted by James Smith of Jordanhill in 1827, and this was managed by Peter MacCallum, the draper. In 1841 a branch of Western Bank of Scotland was set up, but this disappeared and in 1857 its premises and business were taken over by the Clydesdale Bank, whose manager was Mr Orr. Shortly afterwards the premises of the Clydesdale Bank were built where they now are in James Street.

In 1856 the Union Bank of Scotland, under the management of its agent, William Drysdale, the Provost of the town, arrived. In 1861 they moved to their present premises in Colquhoun Square.

Battrum continues by referring to the fact that amongst objects worth a visit in Helensburgh was the cemetery!

Helensburgh being only a recent parish no provision had until recent times been made in connection with a burial ground and the only place of internment was at Rhu, a distance of rather more than 2 miles, but regardless of the distance the parish burying ground at Rhu was inconveniently small and disgracefully kept. At the Helensburgh Kirk Session it had been resolved some eight years ago to erect a cemetery at the east extremity of the town considerably delays had occurred in bringing this to fruition until in the early 1860's when a cemetery was tastefully laid out and enclosed and a superintendent's house built and rules and regulations adopted which will secure its future maintenance and good preservation.

A considerable part of the ground enclosed is devoted to raising nursery plants and flowers which form an interesting feature to visitors and that through order and neatness in which the whole is kept reflects the highest credit on Mr Craig the superintendent. Already one end of the ground is occupied by many very handsome tombstones and placed with great regard to position and order. The locality of the cemetery is good and the soil of a light gravely nature and drained to a great depth is eminently suitable for a cemetery but the only drawback is the inconvenient approach to it.

A continuation of the present line of King Street would lead directly to it but this street is not being fully opened eastward and the access at this time is by Dumbarton Road as far as the Drumfork toll then at the Old Luss Road the distance thereby being nearly doubled. In 1865 there is no trade of any importance carried on in Helensburgh and it is almost entirely dependent on its visitors for its prosperity and growth. This migratory population not only creates a demand for every kind of necessity but is the only means of supplying the want of a class of the population whose time is devoted between boating and fishing.

A number of the adult population are engaged in herring and deep sea fishing for a considerable portion of the year and another part derives its livelihood by attendance on the demands of pleasure and fishing parties during the summer following other callings during the winter. On a quiet summers afternoon the whole bay and loch seem studded with small craft in groups of half a dozen or more at every haunt where fish are traditionally or actually found.

Battrum continues by recording that there are several pleasant strolls and carriage drives in the immediate area and identifies the three principal ones being eastwards towards Dumbarton, westwards along the Gareloch and northwards towards Luss.

The west road along the Gareloch brings the tourists within views of many bits of admirable water scenery, is full of windings and various little bays of the loch and their background studded with villas rising amongst the trees in terraces and crowned with hills like Swiss villages are favourite haunts of sketchers and painters in summer holidays.

To the east on the other hand after leaving Helensburgh the road passes through fine agricultural country where there are few houses save farm homesteads along the way but the farms are in a high state of good management and the land is generally well cultivated.

The road to the north presents a rather steep ascent from the seafront for the first mile but after this is conquered the tourist rapidly reaches the region of the heather and he will not regret his past labours.

Amongst the neucks and corners worth exploring is the turnpike road to Luss now disused and neglected save as its suits the convenience of the farmer through who's lands it may pass. It was once partly a mainland part of communication between the lowlands and the fastnesses of Perth and Stirling and was extensively used in connection with the ferries to the opposite shores of Greenock and Port Glasgow. It was made at the expense of the Duke of Argyll and in Helensburgh chartery is termed as the Duke's Road. His grace is said to have been much displeased at the reaction given to it by those interested, his desire being that it should have taken the general direct of General Wade's road that preceded it and that road after passing Dalligan Farmhouse took the direct of Little Drumfad passing the green burn above the mill damn, and progressed above the Glennan farmhouse to the east bank above Glennan burn.

The old road leads from the east boundary of the town to the farm of Kirkmichael and near this at one time stood the remains of a chapel dedicated to St Michael with certain monastic buildings. The chapel was in existence at the beginning of the 1700's and from old parish records seems to have been used as a place of worship, although it is now difficult to trace its exact site.

There was also another chapel dedicated to St Michael upstream from the Millig Mill, in the area known still as Chapelacre, the ruins of which, the minister recorded in 1839, were still traceable along with that of the associated Hermitage after which the modern day park is named.

Again in 1865 Battrum describes the locality of Row or, Rhue of Connel, as being applicable to the remarkable neck of promontory in the Gareloch which then approached much nearer to Rosneath than now, the insignificance of this title, however, affords no fair criteria by which to judge the locality. Battrum describes the road from Helensburgh to Row as:

The most popular of strolls in the whole neighbourhood and on a summer evening it is crowded with pedestrians and on few days of the year at all hours will you not meet walkers of all classes. The road which is narrow and indifferently preserved leads one along the margin of the Gareloch to the village of Row a distance of about two miles from Helensburgh.

Immediately on passing Helensburgh, Ardencaple Castle and policies appear on the right hand side of the road. The castle is a building of some antiquity and some local historical interest and stands on a rising knoll, defended by an array of stately trees by whose leafy branches it is almost wholly concealed during summer.

The more ancient part of Ardencaple Castle has been added to at various times without due regard to the original designs and if it were not for the clustering ivy which has crept the walls reaching in some places the very eaves it would be rather a dull and unsightly mass of rust stones and mortar.

The policies of Ardencaple are now guarded this is reported in 1865, against all in public intrusion by watches, dogs and placards. The Bosky, dells and silven beauties once accessible to the tourists are now denied to the passing visitor who is denied the ability to enter the road leading to the castle.

A little beyond the castle road separates at a point of land known as Cairndhu and 'Neddy's point' from the policies. This point is in the possession of the Argyll family and here from time immemorial a ferry from the opposite castle of Rosneath has existed and in recent times an obnoxious tollbar has been erected the advantage of which are not nearly so apparent as to those of the ferry. The Cairndhu point is about half an acre of land rising to a considerable height above the level of the loch and crowned by some twenty beech trees whose shade in the summer affords an agreeable lounge to travellers. Except for the tollbar there are now no houses on the point although the traces of foundations of one or two are discernible amongst the grassy surface.

Battrum goes on to recall that one or two cottages exist here within the memory of the current generation, the principal of these being occupied by "Neddy" whose surviving name has distinguished the locality. He was ferryman and fisherman to the Duke of Argyll and seems to have been somewhat of an original. His wife, a little English woman, used to help him daily to launch his boat and waited on the beach for his arrival home in the evening invariably saluting him, as he stepped ashore with "welcome home Neddy. Fish or nay fish".

Battrum continues:

The rocks about this point afforded shelter during the summer to a succession of gangs of tinkers whereby nothing reaches their case but the order of the policeman to move on. They know no higher authority and no purer law other than which can be enforced by the baton society which seems to consider them less privileged and entitled to live and die in the most debased ignorance and idleness.

From this point to Rhu quay, Cairndhu bay or Ardencaple bay as it is sometimes termed forms a beautiful crescent like sweep of about half a mile and the ground ascends gradually from the waters edge to considerable height white and grey villas rising above each other look forth from the overhanging woods down on the loch beneath..

On a calm summer day when the woods are in full foliage, abounding in various tint and shadow and almost screen the houses from view the image in softer tone of the bussow of the waters there is scarcely a more beautiful bit of scenery over which one can linger. At this point but at the further extremity of the bay is Rhu quay.

Chapter 11   The West Highland Railway

The author has endeavoured to present the story contained within this book in chronological sequence but for this chapter only has changed this into one story line embracing the whole period, from the development of railways in 1840 to the present day as much of the development is inter-related over time.

From the 1840's onwards railway mania took over the whole of the United Kingdom, and least of all in Scotland, and many companies were formed to promote railway ideas to Parliament wherein an Act was required to set up a railway line.

Whilst most of the railway promoters were hard-headed businessmen, politics came into play in promoting various schemes or events from local landowners who wanted the railway nowhere near their premises, or those who welcomed it with open arms as it could only bring them prosperity. By the mid 1800's two major companies had emerged. The Caledonian company, formed by Railway Act in 1845, operated principally in the West of Scotland and had established a Callander – Oban line in the 1850's. They shared with most other promoting railway companies a belief that what was required was a central Scottish grand junction and the siting of their station at Callander. What to a latter-day reader might appear incongruous, was their way of keeping options open for plugging into such a network.

The North British Railway Company operated principally in the East of Scotland, but, after it purchased the Edinburgh – Glasgow Railway Company in the 1860's its ambitions towards the West of Scotland became obvious, and rivalry with Caledonian became intense. One example of this is a line from Glasgow to Dumbarton. Even today there are the remnants of two tracks running in parallel past Bowling, Old Kilpatrick, Milton to Dumbarton. It ended there with two separate railway stations currently linked on one line.

Dumbarton East and Dumbarton Central were the termini for separate railway companies back in the 1800's. Caledonian had developed its railway through the Vale of Leven to Balloch and Balloch Pier, and linked a rail line at a later stage from Balloch to Stirling; whereas North British concentrated on a link to Cardross and Helensburgh where they saw scope for a major link with the steamers.

After prolonged debate with the powers in Helensburgh, the idea of running the railway line onto the pier in the centre of the town was dropped. Craigendoran, on the outskirts of the town, was developed in the 1880's and this became very significant in the story of the West Highland Railway Line.

The aspiration of the main companies promoting railways was to create a link to a western harbour and many options were promoted from Oban, Fort William, Mallaig and Roshven, a sheltered bay to the south of Mallaig, which government surveyors felt offered the best option of all locations on the west coast.

Roshven was a classic example of the political inter-play with local land owners and railway promoting companies, but it did not come into being because Professor Blackburn, Emeritus Professor of Mathematics at the University of Glasgow owned the surrounding 60,000 acres. As the new harbour was to be built under the windows of his mansion house, he declared the whole thing abominable. He was supported in his protest by his eminent colleague at the University, Sir William Thompson, Professor of Natural Philosophy, who told the committee of inquiry that he backed his friend's rejection of the scheme on the basis that he had difficulty getting into Roshven in his yacht. The committee seemed to place more faith in Sir William's words than the admiralty's sailing charts which described Roshven as the best harbour on the West of Scotland, but it was abandoned and never developed in any way.

Amongst the many schemes proposed were some which today would seem plainly absurd. One such was a rail link from Whistlefield to Portincaple to bring the fish catches up to the main railway line. It was also proposed at one stage to have a railway line down to Inverary, going over the Rest And Be Thankful. Equally absurd, although promoted on many occasions, was a scheme to put a railway up Ben Nevis, first promoted in 1893 and finally in 1907 after which nothing more was heard.

More practical schemes revolved round the choice of routes towards the North of Scotland, where it would appear the railway companies had their eyes on links with Inverness. There was in existence a Highland Railway Company spreading its tentacles outwards from Inverness, and, naturally, they opposed any potential intrusion into their area.

The major landowners, although often investors in the proposed railway company or indeed sitting on their boards, were very protective of their own areas. An example of this was the Duke of Montrose who, from his seat at the Buchanan Castle, was assured that the line of the proposed railway one mile to the east of Drymen would not be visible from the castle grounds. The Duke insisted that it would be visible from the top of the castle tower and sent his map back to the railway company with an acceptable version pencilled in – a diversion that entailed an impossible rise to a 1,200 foot summit and an equally impossible fall . Special care also had to be taken to avoid Lord Lovat's house in one proposal to put a railway down the eastern side of Loch Lomond, and at Rowardennan the line had to be diverted from the side of Loch Lomond and screened by a curtain of trees from an important shooting lodge.

Not all landowners were hostile to the railway, and one, George Grant McKay of Glen Goy, commented: "At present there is great destitution in some parts of the Western Islands and there is none where there is a railway. Destitution flies away from within a considerable distance of a railway. McKay was in a position to know because he had made a practice of buying up estates where railways were due to pass and selling them on after the railway had been established. An example of this was the way he had brought an estate at Larg for £50,000 and sold it for £100,000 when the railway came.

The foregoing commentary is intended to set the scene of the railway mania in the latter part of the 1800's and any reader wishing to go into much greater detail is referred to the books identified in the bibliography. Now it is, perhaps, time to talk about the West Highland Railway. At the time of writing, it proceeds from Craigendoran through Crianlarich to either Oban or Fort William and then onward to Mallaig, the end of the line and a leading west coast port in its day.

The West Highland line was conceived in a mail coach rumbling along the rough road from Fort William to Kingussie one morning in the late 1880's. In those days the people of Lochaber had to travel 50 miles to Kingussie to reach the Highland Railway. The mail coach left Fort William every day at six am and did not reach Kingussie until 12.20pm. The fare was 13s 6d second class, plus one shilling driver's fee.

Mr Boyd of Fort William was a passenger in the coach and had been very disappointed at the recent failure of the railway companies to bring a track to Fort William. It was at Kingussie, he said afterwards, that:

> I first thought of doing all that lay in my power to get a railway to Fort William. I had been on a journey to Banffshire and was the only passenger by coach on that particular morning, and on going into the Hotel at Kingussie I was surprised to find the Scotsman for that day already there which demonstrated to me the capability of the railway to deliver a quick service. Thinking about the situation at a slightly later stage I thought of the backwardness of Lochaber and how far behind Kingussie, Inverness and Oban it was and I might tell you frankly that when I thought of these things I wept.

On his return to Lochaber, Boyd got in touch with George Malcolm, the factor of Invergoy, and declared his plan which at this time did not include a serious scheme to reach Inverness but merely an attempt to link Lochaber and Fort William with the south, giving an outlet to the western sea.

The factor shared Boyd's enthusiasm, and the two men obtained the moral and financial support of landowners. According to Boyd, The Caledonian Company was invited to build the railway but would have nothing to do with it. The North British when sounded out showed a lively interest and *The Scotsman reported*

> We have here an endeavour to mark an era that the development of the Highlands, access to markets, has hereto been deemed the one thing needful to raise into activity our island populations who live near seas teeming with fish. The people of these districts – whether lairds, tenants or crofters – are too poor to provide capital for such works and a return in dividend is so doubtful that the subscription list might be viewed as scarce on the stock exchange.

In 1889 the separately constituted West Highland Railway Company, backed by the North British Railway Company, produced a statement of estimated revenues which covered the proposed line from Craigendoran to Fort William, a distance of 101 miles at a cost of £617,780. After factoring in the projected revenues from many sources, including movements from the three leading distilleries in Fort William, the transport of coal to Fort William, the movement of livestock south from scattered communities, and a dividend of four and a half percent per annum, there would be a small working profit each year.

As feudalism had robbed the railway company of the outlet to the western seas at Roshven, one of the main reasons for the company's existence was in question. True enough, Fort William was on salt water but only by an accident of geography, and Loch Linnhe was far from the fishing grounds. The fishing villages of the west were 40 miles overland from Fort William, but close to 100 miles by water. The West Highland, if it was to survive, would not let its terminal remain at Fort William. The railway had to get to the sea, if only to channel fish traffic to the mainline. That alone would give the line a chance of paying its way.

In March 1892 the government sent a committee to the West Highlands to inquire into the need for transport and harbours. These gentlemen found that the landowners who had been so obstructive in the recent past were now inclined to modify their views. The investigating committee picked Mallaig Bay as the best place for a railway terminal and suggested that a breakwater be built to enclose 30 acres of water. A connecting line should be constructed to the West Highland at Banavie, a short spur north from Fort William to the Caledonian canal. The committee considered that such a railway built in extremely difficult and sparsely populated country would have no chance of paying its way and recommended that the treasury make a payment of £100,000 to the cost of the project. Meanwhile, the North British Railways separately had reached the conclusion that the Mallaig extension would not pay and the directors were not prepared to recommend its construction to their shareholders, unless the government gave adequate financial guarantees.

The West Highland Railway Company promoted its West Highland railway (Mallaig) extension bill in 1894. At the same time The Treasury was empowered to pay grants and dividends to the builders and holders of Mallaig extension stock which gave rise to a quite separate West Highland Railway Guarantee Bill.

This Bill faced much opposition as Parliament by and large did not know or care where Fort William and Mallaig were situated. Eventually opposition was overcome and the Guarantee Bill came up in Parliament again in 1896. This time it was passed with terms that the Treasury underwrite to shareholders three percent on the £260,000 of the Mallaig extension capital and make a grant of £30,000 towards the £40.000 cost of a pier at Mallaig.

There were two separate contracts, one covering the route from Craigendoran to Fort William along the Garelochside, the route not identified by any other railway company wishing to push north and which was probably the key feature in this proposal gaining credence and parliamentary assent. The contractors were Lucas and Aird from Glasgow and construction began on 23rd October, 1889. The line to Fort William was open in August 1894. The separate and standalone West Highland Railway Company was floated with a share capital of £540,000 and debentures at £180,000 which were taken up by many individuals and landowners but in substantial part by the North British Railway Company who contracted to operate the line on behalf of The Highland Railway Company.

The extension from Fort William to Mallaig was contracted by R. McAlpine and Sons and construction began in January 1897. In spite of severe labour shortages, it was opened in April 1901. Sir Robert McAlpine was known in the industry as "concrete" Bob for his much-preferred method of building, using concrete. It is said that the Mallaig line, which uses it extensively instead of dressed stone, considerably kept the cost down and took the construction industry a significant step forward in the development and use of this material.

An interesting anecdote McAlpine's youngest son Malcolm who was assistant construction manager at the age of 19. The working of rock on the Mallaig extension was proving very difficult due to its hardness; compressed air drills were making minimal progress. When Malcolm was in Helensburgh visiting a dentist and lying in the chair having his teeth drilled, he wondered how the drill was powered and asked the dentist to explain it to him. The dentist advised that he made the drill work by pressing on a knob on the floor with his foot, operating a valve in a water pipe under the floor causing a flow of high pressure water to spray on a rotary turbine which provided the power.

Malcolm went back to his engineering team on the site They built a water turbine which ran at 900 r.p.m. By the end of 1897 the turbine was working day and night within two miles of cuttings and tunnels.

The engineers reported that the turbine was doing four times the amount of work of the steam compressor which it had replaced.

Work on the Craigendoran – Fort William contract was overseen by engineers Forman and McCall, who had a formidable record of railway building, and would direct and control the railway builders. On the 23rd October, 1889, a party of railway and contractor's men went to a spot opposite the Glen Nevis Distillery, outside Fort William. In the presence of half the population, Lord Abbinger took a silver spade and dug the first sod. That was the end of the ceremonial and thereafter followed the gruelling task of building the West Highland Railway which was to continue for a further five-year period. The inaccessibility of much of the country was the most daunting feature. The armies of navvies required for large-scale civil engineering had to be assembled and camps established. For administrative purposes the work was divided into Section one, from Craigendoran to Crianlarich, and Section two, from Crianlarich to Fort William. Construction began at five points. The southern-most camp was at Craigendoran, with easy access by rail and sea. Arrochar, at the head of Loch Long, was the site of the second camp. The third was at Inverglus on Loch Lomond, three miles south of Ardlui, where a pier was built to which heavy materials were brought in boats and barges. Section two was divided into two parts, Crianlarich to Gorton and Gorton to Fort William. Whereas on railway one no point was more than eight miles from a base camp, on railway two there was no permanent camp between Crianlarich and Fort William, although at an early stage a base camp was established at Inverauran, the northern-most point reached by the coast road. Along the whole project all the camps were linked to headquarters in Helensburgh by private telephone, where a close check could be kept on progress. Among the materials ordered for delivery by sea at Helensburgh and Fort William and by rail to Tyndrum were 12,000 tons of rails and 81,000 Scots fir sleepers.

Pressure was put on the contractors to employ more native

Highlanders, rather than imported Irish navvies,. It was soon established that many could not afford to travel from their homes to the contract and a recruitment programme was put in place which would pay the passages of those who could not afford them. Some 300 Highlanders were induced to work on the scheme out of a total navvy population of around about 5,000.

As work progressed from the Craigendoran end, the sensitivities of local residents occasionally came into play. Cutting the track up to what is now Helensburgh Upper Station was a substantial exercise and the wealthy gentry of Upper Helensburgh complained that they could see the railway from their houses. They asked the railway company to build their boundary walls three feet higher. Eventually a compromise was reached and the railway company paid a sum to the "wealthy gentry of Upper Helensburgh" of £150 for them to build their own walls.

The broad construction policy was to balance embankment volume against cuttings and to use excavated stone to build the piers of bridges, thus saving significant costs of purchasing and transporting materials. The first two miles from Craigendoran to Helensburgh Upper involved a 1 in 58 climb, partly on a mile-long embankment, 30 feet high, using some 140,000 cubic yards of material out of cuttings further along the line.

The engineers found it necessary to build only one tunnel – that on Loch Lomond-side 47 yards long. An example of how the cost of tunnelling was avoided is at Rhu where the railway was taken across Whistlers Glen by laying down two long culverts to carry the water below and filling 57 feet of rock material above these to carry the line across the glen.

To service the increasingly developing, gentrified residential areas along the Gareloch side, stations were strategically positioned, although it was reported that concerns by the landowners caused them to acquire more land and push the line of the railway further up the hill than had originally been planned.

With the line starting at Craigendoran, there were, for some time, two stations at that point, one servicing the steamer piers, the other, the start of the Highland Line. Thus it was possible to arrive at Craigendoran by steamer from the Clyde estuary, transfer to a West Highland train and travel to Fort William and Mallaig merely by walking some 40 or so paces.

For the first section of the line along the Gareloch, stations were positioned within residential communities at Helensburgh Upper, Rhu and Shandon, which was also designed to service the Shandon Hydropathic Spa. The proprietors had promised to expand the spa when the railway came, but they ended up in dispute with the railway company who would not provide the service to Glasgow that the Hydropathic Company demanded.

At Glen Douglas a petition by the farmers in the glen for a siding halt to assist the movement of their livestock, was successful. In later years Glen Douglas became a major area for storing armaments. In the Railway Act of 1889 the railway company had undertaken to build a station at Portincaple, a hamlet beside Loch Long several hundred feet below the railway. It was only after the protestation of local residents that this was constructed at Whistlefield and opened in 1896.

Stations were erected at Arrochar and Tarbet, Ardlui and at Crianlarich, where a line crossed over the existing line of the Callander and Oban facility, diverted north by the creation of a second, upper, station at Tyndrum. It then progressed to Bridge of Orchy, Gortan, Rannoch, Corrour, Tulloch, Roy Bridge, Spean Bridge and Fort William, where the railway ran through the town to the pierhead. After its installation the town realised this was a monstrous piece of town planning as it cut the town off from the foreshore. It was not until 1975 that a new terminus on the outskirts of town was opened, replacing the original station in the centre. The contract for the Fort William – Mallaig extension continued, albeit with much construction difficulty, and the extension was opened in April 1901.

Progress had been made in 1897 with the opening of a spur link from the Highland Railway onto the Callander and Oban line, thus facilitating co-operation between the two companies in providing a more seamless service. It was not until 1965 that the Callander to Crianlarich link was finally closed.

For much of its length the Highland Line was single-track, but there were passing points at a number of stations, including Helensburgh Upper, Rhu, Garelochhead, Crianlarich and Rannoch, amongst others, but care had to be taken to ensure that trains did not appear on the same single track from opposite directions. Signalling developments were all-important in this respect.

Attracting tourism had always been one of the objectives of the Railway Company, and it would appear that the volume of traffic that developed to the great sporting estates of the Highlands was much bigger than originally anticipated. The Glorious Twelfth was still a key date in the British calendar of social events and the trunk lines from the South to Scotland carried the heaviest passenger traffic on the tenth and eleventh of August each year. The sport was first class and, to accommodate the great demand, many sporting estates were developed adjacent to the railway and sufficient volume developed, particularly at Rannoch, Corrour and Gorton, that during the sporting season from August until October extra clerkesses had to be employed to oversee the despatch of grouse and deer to the markets in the south, as well as receiving the sportsmen.

This was but one example of the employment created by the railway line and in these modern times it is difficult to imagine that most of these stations had a stationmaster and subordinate staff. Until the 1960's Helensburgh upper station employed five staff, a stationmaster, two signalmen and two porters. This continued until the Beeching era of railway rationalisation when many of these stations became unmanned. It is also interesting to note that the first sleeping car service from Kings Cross. London, to Fort William was introduced in 1901 for the summer period only. In 1929 a significant step forward took place with sleeping cars operating throughout the year, with restaurant cars on appropriately-timed trains.

The Second World War brought many changes. Because of the dangers to the south coast ports the government of the day identified a number of safe ports, the maximum distance from the European theatre of war. Faslane bay on the Gareloch was identified as one of these. By 1941 jetties had been built and 15 large cranes installed, creating a facility which could accommodate five large ships. A double railway line was taken from Croy, between Rhu and Shandon, on a steeply-falling gradient to the new port in the Faslane Bay. The branch was worked by Royal Engineer railway-operating troops on military principles.

From the opening of the port in May 1942 until August 1945, the Faslane branch received 65 passenger trains and 105,000 loaded wagons. To help in the handling of this traffic, passing loop and signalling accommodation was provided at Faslane junction, a temporary station disbanded after the war. At Helensburgh Upper the loops were extended, and a new marshalling yard was brought into operation at Craigendoran in the area of recovered land between Craigendoran and Ardmore Point.

After the war the facilities were used as a ship breaking yard and the railways continued to play a vital role in taking away the scrap metal . This continued until the 1980's when the metal industry plummeted. The lines were removed and the land used for further development of the Faslane submarine base. The 1990's huge submarine shiplift is built in approximately the area of main occupation of the Faslane port in earlier times.

During post-war years the viability of many of the stations on the lower part of the Highland Line was brought into question. In 1956 Rhu was closed, although it opened again as an un-staffed halt in 1960. But in 1964 during the Beeching rationalisation era Craigendoran on the West Highland Line, Rhu, Shandon, Whistlefield and Glen Douglas closed, although the latter is still used by the Ministry of Defence as a marshalling area for the storage of armaments in Glen Douglas.

The line showed small but steady growth in the revenues in the earlier years but never climbed out of the red once working expenses had been paid. The North British Railway had to dip into its coffers to make up the interest on the guaranteed West Highland stock. For example, in 1899 this cost North British £34,000.

Maintenance costs on the new railways were light at first but increased with the passing years, and North British shareholders became restive over the West Highland. Their chairman lamented in 1907: "I will not venture to prophesy whether the West Highland Line will ever pay a return." After a few years of financial engineering on the 31st December, 1908, the 142 miles of track from Craigendoran to Mallaig passed to the ownership of the North British Railway Company, representing an investment over the years of £2,375,000.

After the Second World War a significant development was the creation of the Loch Sloy hydro-electric power scheme which brought an increase in traffic to the line. Large water pipes were constructed down from the hilltops and the railway line was diverted for about a quarter of a mile to allow the construction of a bridge to carry the track over the pipelines. At the same time Inveruglas station was constructed close to the site of the turbine house to serve the camp where a large part of the labour force was quartered. A halt was also established in Glen Falloch. Each day prisoners of war living in a camp on the site of what is now the Helensburgh Hermitage Academy, and also a camp at Faslane, were picked up by train which then collected British labourers at Arrochar and Tarbet, dropping them all off at Inveruglas and Glen Falloch as required. These stations were removed when the power scheme was completed. It is said that the prisoners of war carved interesting legends in the stone work at the top of the Glen Sloy dam and these are there to this day, recording the individuality of German prisoners of war.

Whilst the transportation and living conditions of the navvies constructing the railway were bleak and difficult in the extreme, the staff employed by the railway company suffered to almost the same degree. Many were the complaints to the railway company who in many instances had not honoured their original promises to provide suitable accommodation.

Linesmen, stationmasters, signalmen and engineers had all been tempted from their more southern habitats to work on the railway, with inducement of approximately the same wages and free accommodation. This attracted many brave souls and their families. Many houses were not completed on time and at a number of stations the staff lived temporarily in the station building. Education was a significant problem, and beyond Crianlarich an old railway carriage was mounted on the platform at Gorton and used as a school. The children were moved up and down the line by trains which stopped wherever there was a child to be collected. By the same principle and process the provisions required by these lonely families were obtained, either by the company putting supplies on the train to be delivered, or by the individuals making a trip to the end of the line to do their own shopping. These were cold and lonely times for the families.

The last part of the Craigendoran – Fort William line to be completed was that over Rannoch Moor where very substantial problems were encountered. Towards the end of construction it was discovered that north of Rannoch Station a depression was not capable of being forded by tipping material, the depth of peat being too great. A 1,000 foot, nine-span viaduct had to be built. The moor swallowed everything it was offered, materials and more particularly money. By the summer of 1893 the promoters in their office in Princes Street, Edinburgh, realised that the authorised capital would not cover the construction costs of the line. The financial crisis that ensued had become so acute that is was only overcome when Mr J H Renton, an investor, one of the directors of the West Highland Railway Company, gave part of his private fortune to save the situation. The help of a fine summer saved it and the last length of rail was dropped into position on September 5th, 1893. Mr Renton was given the privilege of driving the last spike. The railway navvies were so grateful for Mr Renton's gesture that they manhandled a huge boulder to the north end of Rannoch Station and out of it sculpted an excellent head of Renton, using only the tools of their trade. This can be seen on Rannoch Station to this day.

Chapter 12   AD 1900 – 2000

Second World War – Faslane Port – Faslane Development – Cinemas –
Property Developments – Road Developments

The motor road was a recent development, though in 1909 the advent of the car caused a bridge to be built over the Leggie at Magiscroft on the county boundary, where previously there had only been a ford. In 1923 there were only 55 miles of road in Dunbartonshire with a tarmacadam surface. Road competition with the railways started with the electric tramway. The first, to Dalmuir, was laid by Glasgow Corporation in 1903, and Dunbartonshire tramway service formed in 1908, linking Balloch and Dalmuir, via the west bank of the Leven. Motor buses started in the area from about 1920 with small undertakings.

The First World War brought little interruption to the civilian way of life, but the second; '39 to '45 war had dramatic effects. The population of Dunbartonshire were extremely generous in heart and spirit in tending to the homeless. The women folk, often with a husband, son or daughter in the forces or engaged in essential war-work, voluntarily took into their homes, or had billeted on them, the evacuees from the Channel Islands, London and towns on the South Coast of England. Then, with the county already heavily burdened, there were the unforgettable nights of March 13 and 14, 1941, when German bombs rained down on Clydebank, Old Kilpatrick, Bowling, Duntocher and Hardgate. On both nights raids by enemy planes continued from dusk till dawn. Damage to many of the war work factories was negligible, compared to the destruction of dwelling houses, shops and churches.

The population of the Clydebank area of over 50,000 immediately before the conflict dropped to a little over 2,000. By the morning of

March 14 close on 20,000 people had found their own way or been transported to rest centres. It was from the need for reconstruction of Clydebank that many communities, particularly in the Vale of Leven, were developed as an alternative to re-building the old Clydebank tenements. This accounted for the transfer of a significant part of the population to the rural areas on a permanent basis.

Greenock did not escape the ravages of war, for enemy bombers attacked on the nights of the 6th and 7th May, 1941. Over the two nights 280 people were killed and over 1,200 injured, many seriously. The numbers would have been much higher had not many people left the town after the first night's raid to camp on the moors and surrounding areas. Some people who had gone to rest centres after being bombed out on the first night were made homeless for the second time when several of them were hit during the second night.

Whilst Faslane Bay had been recognised and used for centuries as a deep-water anchorage, it was the beginning of the Second World War that it came into its own. The War Office held a strategic review in 1940 in anticipation that southern and east coasts ports would be easy targets for hostile bombing. They looked for safe ports outside the range of these activities. Eventually the Gareloch, a deep sheltered enclosure with ample manoeuvring room, was identified as the prime preference for a military port. It was decided that it would be built in Faslane Bay, partly in view of the potential link to an excellent railway system and the convenience of significant centres of population within travelling distance.

It was estimated that the port could be constructed at a cost of approximately £1.5 million and work started in August 1940. By February 1941 some 1,000 men were engaged in the building of six berths. Work was progressing well, despite the lack of barges and tugs and problems with dredging at the narrows of Rhu. The port was officially opened in August 1942. Each berth was each capable of handling vessels of up to a 33 feet draft. With 36 onshore cranes and a

150 ton floating crane, a 35,000 ton battle ship could be berthed and over 1,500 railway goods wagons could be accommodated in the sidings.

Whilst Faslane was the core of naval activity in the Clyde Estuary during the war, the whole estuary became an area for receiving and assembling convoys for onward journeys to the Channel ports, Africa and the Mediterranean theatre of war. The whole Clyde maritime operation was controlled from a house on Mary Mount in Gourock, on a hillside offering a fine view of the Firth of Clyde. During the war 52 million tons of cargo were handled and around four million troops embarked or disembarked. Five hundred million tons of shipping passed through the estuary. One of the cargoes handled was water from Loch Thom, located in the hills behind Greenock, and needed for the American forces invasion of North Africa.

A significant part of the lower Clyde's contribution to the Second World War effort revolved around the Blackburn Aircraft Company and their factory adjacent to the Rock in Dumbarton. It was a happy coincidence that, in the mid-1930's when the government decided to build armaments factories in the north and west, out of range of air attack from mainland Europe, the Dumbarton shipbuilders, Denny's, were seeking to diversify into aircraft industry.

An agreement was announced in early 1937 for a factory to be built at Barge Park, Dumbarton, for the construction of aircraft for the expanding Royal Air Force. It is a little known fact that Denny Brothers had built in 1910 one of the world's first helicopters at Dumbarton. Whilst its trials were very successful, the design was not developed, largely because of the outbreak of the First World War, although during that war they did build 150 BE2 training and reconnaissance planes for Royal Flying Corps.

Construction of the new factory began in early 1937 and, such was the speed of construction, that the operation commenced in October of the same year. Very quickly a workforce of 4,000 was employed, a slipway built to the river and a railway siding in the factory. The first completed aircraft rolled off the assembly line in October 1939, one month after war was declared.

The work at times was varied, with repairs, modifications and component manufacturing, interspersed amongst aircraft construction. The first work was for the assembly, upgrading and maintenance of 'The Shark', a torpedo/spotter/reconnaissance bi-plane. The Botha, a short/medium range bomber, started to come off the production line in October 1939 and over a 17-month period some 200 were produced. The design was superseded and by 1943 the Botha was out of active service. The land-based planes were transported from the factory by a special barge, one at a time, up river to the Abbotsinch Airfield.

By early 1940 the need for seaplanes to counter the threat from U-boats was established and the Short Sunderland was the model of choice. Initially it was built in the Short Brothers in Rochester, Kent, but, because of its vulnerability to raids from mainland Europe, it was decided to expand production at Dumbarton and the first plane was completed by October 1940.

By the time the final and 250th Sunderland had been built in Dumbarton, it was 1945 and peace had returned. This was no mean feat, as each one was 85 feet long with a wingspan of 122 feet, as high as a three-storey tenement building, and crammed with radio and electronic gear. It is amazing that the factory produced one per week.

The bombing raids on the 5th and 6th of May, 1941, nearly had disastrous results for the factory, although the prime targets were the Greenock shipyards. One landmine landed on the roof of the final assembly hall and hung inside when its parachute caught in the roof structure. Fortunately it did not explode and was quickly de-fused.

After production of a seaplane, it was the practice to tow the plane, slowly and with difficulty, to the Marine Aircraft Experimental Establishment at Rhu Hangars. The modern hangars now on the Rhu foreshore were a replacement in the 1980's of the original and larger ones. During the war the hangars were the headquarters of the north-western branch of Coastal Command, with some seaplanes being based and operating from them. Other planes were delivered to Coastal Command at the hangars for testing and onward despatch to other Coastal Command bases. At the start of production, the Clyde Navigation Trust feared that the river walls would be damaged by high speed taxiing and so a long and tedious tow to Rhu barges was used, until Group Captain Flood arrived. He started the engines on the slipway, slammed the throttles open and taxied at high speed down the Blackburn private channel. Becoming airborne just as he met the main channel, he banked to avoid the Langbank Hills and flew down the estuary to land on the water by Rhu Hangars. Thereafter all seaplanes were moved this way and a fine sight they provided down the estuary.

After the war a number of planes were designed, but only three were adopted and only parts of these were, for a period, produced at Dumbarton. Perhaps the best known of these was the Buccaneer, which remained in service until 1992. The last work at the factory included pre fabricated houses, but it never established a clearly-defined product range and closed in 1960.

In April 1940 the worst accident during the wartime period of Clyde activity occurred when the French destroyer *Maille Breze*, which was lying in a crowded anchorage at the Tail of the Bank, making preparations for her next journey. Shortly before 3.00p.m. the area was shattered by huge explosion when a live torpedo, which had been raised for routine maintenance, slipped from its tube and exploded as it hit the deck. The explosion ripped a gaping hole in the deck and starboard side of the ship and started a fire, which swept throughout the destroyer fanned by strong south-west winds.

The anchorage immediately burst into life, with vessels of all shapes rushing to the assistance of the stricken vessel. She began to settle by the stern and a number of survivors were picked up. The skippers of these vessels exposed themselves to considerable danger from the continuous exploding of shells and ammunition on board the destroyer. The ship sank five hours later taking with her 28 of the crew. Her mast protruded from the surface of the river until the wreck was removed in 1954.

As the war progressed it became apparent that all the Atlantic coast ports were becoming outside the range of bombing hostilities and work flowed southwards from Faslane nearer the Channel ports where the invasion of Europe was being planned. From the latter part of 1943 it was recognised that Faslane had significant surplus capacity.

At the end of the war, in April 1945, the War Office decided that the site should be leased to a ship-breaking company. Metal Industries Limited were the favoured choice, with their offer to lease the site and purchase the plant in July 1946 for £102,500.

There was a continuous supply of ships to be broken up. The Gareloch was used as a holding area for redundant ships. Amongst others which were scrapped at Faslane were HMS Vanguard and the liner Aquitania, together with, in the 1950's battleships, two aircraft carriers and many other large vessels. The majority of the workers on the Faslane site were Polish, who had been displaced by the Second World War and lived on site in the former army huts.

These activities continued through to 1981 with the scrap metal being taken by railway line linking onto the West Highland Railway to the centres of steel production.

Large areas of land on the foreshore between Ardmore Point and Craigendoran had been recovered during the war and used as substantial railway sidings to store material waiting movement to Faslane port for shipment. For many years after the end of hostilities wagons and carriages were to be seen on these sidings, but by 1965 the Ardmore Steel Company was still busy burning old carriages and selling the metal as scrap. At the same time Dumbarton County Council was trying to have the site rezoned from agricultural to industrial use, but the Secretary of State rejected this proposal. One legacy of this activity is that the land was found to be contaminated with asbestos and the land where the sidings were located remains undisturbed. In 1968 The British Steel Corporation announced proposals to create an iron ore terminal at this point with follow-up plans to construct a large steel complex on the site. In 1972 the South of Scotland Electricity Board revealed that it was seriously looking at Ardmore and also Kilcreggan as possible locations for a nuclear power station. By 1975 Ardmore and Portkil were under scrutiny in relation to oil construction sites, but again there were reprieves and no development took place, although you only have to look over the river to Port Glasgow to realise how close Ardmore and its surrounding area might have come to forming part of industrial Scotland.

From the 1960's onwards, the southern part of the Faslane site was used as a service area for submarines. At this time there were minimal buildings on the shore. Various vessels, ending with HMS Maidstone, were moored at the jetty acting as "mother ships", with the submarines being serviced on the offshore side.

During the early 1960's nuclear submarines became a reality, and agreements were made with America to purchase some of these and their related systems. A search for a suitable base was instituted, ending with the choice of Faslane. Development of the base at Faslane commenced in March 1962 and by the following year the first nuclear powered submarine H.M.S. Dreadnought joined the squadron in Faslane. In May 1963 the government placed orders for the Polaris submarines and major works began at Faslane immediately.

Work continued to develop berthing and shore facilities, and by 1968 the base was sufficiently developed for HMS Maidstone to conclude its role as support ship for the submarine flotilla.

The development in the area at this time was significant, and in 1968 the new Churchill Estate Community Centre, supermarket and Drumfork Club were opened.

In 1969 730 houses on the Churchill estate were handed over to the Ministry of Defence. By June 1969 the complement on the base was 6,500 civilian and service personnel, divided between Faslane and Coulport. With their dependants, this influx had a substantial effect on the previously tranquil, rural town of Helensburgh, which now became very-much based and reliant on naval activities.

From the 1950's onwards a new and second era in the history of Helensburgh had developed.

In the 175 years since its formation, Helensburgh had grown slowly and in a rather gentle way as a residential area for the more wealthy people in the West of Scotland. The development of transportation progressively encouraged this, firstly with the steamers, then with the lower railway line. In the early 1900's, with the Highland Line running through the upper part of Helensburgh, the town became very much a commuter town for Glasgow.

Alongside the grand houses, the lower end of the town developed for the tradesmen and services which were a necessary part of what then was a fairly self-contained community.

Municipal housing was introduced into Helensburgh in 1919, when the site at the west end of King Street behind the then Fernigair House was allocated for the building of Ardencaple Quadrant. The decision to build these houses was mainly to provide accommodation for men returning home from the 1st World War who wanted to marry and settle down but could not afford to buy homes of their own. It was ruled that the cost of a two-apartment house must not exceed £358, and a three-apartment house £412. This made the architects reduce the height of the walls, cancel fireplaces in back bedrooms and eliminate parapet walls and ash pits.

The flowering trees, which adorn many Helensburgh streets when in blossom during May, were planted by Doctor Ewing Hunter just before the 1st World War to commemorate his time of service on the town council. The first trees he planted were edible cherry, but this proved too much of a temptation to the school children and they were destroyed. He then planted flowering cherry trees and that is what we see today. Originally he had planted Laburnum trees up Sinclair Street, but one of the small boys in the town ate a pod and almost died. They were uprooted and replaced with flowering cherries.

Argyll Street had significant claim to fame in that two of the most memorable residents of the town were born in this street. John Logie Baird, the inventor of television, was born in 'The Lodge', and, across the street in 'Fairyknowe', Jack Buchanan, matinee idol and star of stage and screen, was born. Both boys went to Larchfield School and were great personal friends.

In 1935 the burgh surveyor laid out an idealistic garden city development outside the eastern outskirts of the town to house families formerly housed in sub-standard tenements in the town centre. Three blocks, which remain, were built on Kirkmichael Road, adjacent to Kirkmichael Farm, on which the remains of a very early chapel had been located. With the outbreak of the Second World War, this development was halted, but after the war further developments of tenements and cottages were made in Ben Buie Drive and Buchanan Road. Regrettably the embryonic garden suburb was absorbed into the sprawling urbanisation to the east of the town.

The town developed slowly and very little redevelopment had taken place over the first 175 years, being little more than half its present size by 1950. During the 1960's the development of the naval base at Faslane and Ministry of Defence depot at Coulport brought large numbers of workers and staff into the area. Developments took place in many areas to accommodate the very substantial influx of population. In 1950 there was virtually no development at all to the east of the railway line, other than Osbournes Pig Farm, and the golf clubhouse which were effectively in the countryside. Adjacent to the Golf Club in 1952 Colquhoun Estates started to offer land to feu. One resident in Lennox Drive recently recounted that Luss Estates endeavoured to force him to feu one acre, whereas he only wanted half an acre. The price was £8 to buy the feu, with a rental of £8 per annum. That later became very expensive when 20 years later he had to buy out the feudal title for £60! At that time land did not sell very readily.

In a short period during the late 1960's and 1970's the whole of

Colgrain, Churchill housing estate, Clyde Arran Estate, Glade Estate, much of Kirkmichael and on the west end of town the naval housing surrounding the old ruins of Ardencaple Castle were built. In the upper part of the town, the area to the right of Sinclair Street was developed and on the left estates were developed – Black Hill Drive, Kennedy Drive and those general areas. In the west side of the town the area surrounding Duchess Park, Strathclyde Court, Edward Drive and inter-connected developments took place. At the extreme west end of the town smaller developments took place in Kathleen Park and Dalmore Crescent.

The rate of change during the late 1960's through to the early 1990's was truly phenomenal, and possibly can only be fully appreciated by looking at the picture stories of 'before and after' which are readily available in the recently published book "Helensburgh Past and Present" (see bibliography).

Henry Bell's original Baths Hotel, latterly known as the Queens Hotel, was the social centre of the well-to-do Helensburghers until the early 1980's. It had an excellent cocktail bar and restaurant. In the early 1980's the hotel closed and was developed into residential flats.

One of the oldest churches in Helensburgh was St. Bride's, a stone structure on Princes Street. The first minister was John Baird, father of John Logie Baird, the pioneer of television. The church became disused by the mid 1980's and was knocked down and the site redeveloped as a library and adjoining residential flats. The stonework from the demolished church was used to form the foundation of the proposed industrial estate on the outskirts of Helensburgh at the top of Sinclair Street.

The fate of the three cinemas in Helensburgh makes sorry reading. The Plaza Ballroom opened in 1911 as a picture palace constructed of wood and corrugated iron. By 1926, the competition from the other cinemas in the town was too much for the old cinehouse and it closed. After a time it reopened as the Plaza Ballroom or 'Honky Tonk' which was a popular rendezvous for British and American servicemen during the Second World War. The council eventually purchased the old Plaza building and a block of flats for local authority tenants was erected on the site in 1970.

The Tower Cinema, which opened in the lower east corner of Colquhoun Square in 1927, continued for many years. As recently as 1955, the management brought Cinemascope to the Tower, but it was forced to close after massive storm damage during the 1968 hurricane. It did not reopen and was demolished in 1973. Shortly thereafter a block of flats with the Royal Bank of Scotland and other shops beneath was built.

La Scala Cinema was opened in James Street in 1913, equipped with the latest technology, including 'tip up seats' and boxes. In the early 1980's La Scala was converted into a cinema, snooker hall and entertainment arcade. These all eventually closed in the early 1990's and the building stood in a locked up condition for many years.

Without doubt the biggest changes which took place were along the seafront. Up to 1950 the pier was a standalone jetty, with buildings on the end for the shelter of passengers. Steamers called regularly. At the landward end was a stone arch with offices and toilets. Alongside was a seawater open-air swimming pool which had been gifted to the town by Bailie Andrew Buchanan in 1928.

By the end of the 1930's the pier at Helensburgh had deteriorated to such an extent that only local steamers called. Silting brought closure in 1952. It was re-dredged by the Clydeport Authority in the late 1980's, and the paddle steamer 'Waverley' included the pier on its summer schedules. With privatisation of Clydeport in the early 1990's dredging ceased, and, by 2001, the 'Waverley' has difficulty docking at low tide.

In the mid 1970's the seashore to the east of the swimming pond, along to the site of the old town church was infilled and formed initially a car park. But in 1977 a modern indoor pool was opened on the recovered land. The indoor and outdoor pools were open in parallel for about another year when the old outdoor pool was filled in and landscaped as a children's play area.

It the late 1970's further land reclamation, almost to the end of the pier, formed a huge asphalt car park. At the Clyde Street end stands a modern public house which has been developed from The Granary, one of the earliest buildings in Helensburgh,. It was built originally on the foreshore with docking facilities alongside for moving grains in and out. It subsequently became a garage for MacFarlanes Gareloch motor service, probably the earliest motor bus company in Dunbartonshire. Subsequently it became a restaurant, before lying empty during the 1970's. Thereafter it was made into the public house we see today.

Looking at Helensburgh beaches in the town's bi-centenary year, it is perhaps difficult to believe that these were once covered by golden sands. There are many people around at the time of writing who can remember the period up to the Second World War when the sands in the west bay were ideal for building sand castles and for donkey rides. The sand in the east bay was drier and softer and ideal for 'running your toes through'.

The sand disappeared little by little, year by year, after the war, one theory being that, as Rhu Narrows and the offshore channel were dredged for naval purposes, the current sucked the sand away. Indeed, there are shallows and sandbanks some 100 yards offshore

In the middle of the estuary can be seen a wreck lying on the bank in the middle of the river. This is the hull of the Greek boat 'Captayannis' which in January 1972 had arrived at the Tail of the Bank with a cargo of sugar from Lorenzo Marques in Portuguese East Africa. She had dropped anchor prior to off-loading her cargo in Greenock, but a severe gale hit the West Coast of Scotland with winds in excess of 60mph. The ship began to drag her anchor, prompting her captain to order 'steam up' and head towards the Gareloch for shelter.

However, before he could get sufficient power the 'Captayannis' collided with the anchor chain of a BP tanker 'British Light' and the anchor chain ripped a gaping hole in the port side of the ship which began to fill with water so quickly that the pumps could not cope. As a number of small boats arrived to render assistance, the 'Captayannis' grounded on the sandbank in the middle of the river and the crew of 25 were taken off by the small boats without injury. The ship became the centre of a commercial wrangle between the parties, resulting in the failure to salvage her. It was anticipated that the cost of doing so was more than the value of the wreck to be recovered.

Two key pieces of redevelopment which took place during the 1960's and 70's relate to mansions to the west of the town – Cairndhu and Ferniegair House. Cairndhu had been built in 1871 and is now a nursing home. In the grounds were built bungalows and flats, leaving the gothic building designed by William Lieper standing in the centre of the site. Immediately on the right hand side of Cairndhu was Ferniegair House, the beautiful home of the Kidston family, which had been built in the 1870's. It was purchased by a local firm of builders in the 1960's, demolished and the ground cleared. A smart housing estate, accessed through Camsail Avenue, is built on the site. The boundary at the rear on Princes Street is still recognised by the coachman's lodge which has been enlarged, modernised and sold as a private house. It is now called The Stables.

Further along towards Rhu, on the corner of Rhu Road Higher, is Dalmore House, built in 1873. During the late 1960's the house was converted into flats and a modern executive development built around the grounds.

To the rear of these properties stood Ardencaple Castle, still lived in as a family home after the Second World War. The building was demolished in 1957 and only the single tower has been retained as a housing for navigational lights, whilst the naval housing estate was built around the location of the castle during the 1960's.

In the upper part of the town, Chapelacre House stood in six acres of ground and was accessed from Sinclair Street, its rear boundary on East Abercromby Street, or its front boundary on Victoria Road. This property was lived in until 1973 when it was vacated and the whole put on the market for £50,000. Due to planning restrictions and preserved trees, the grounds lay empty and derelict until the middle of the 1980's when the modern executive development was built.

The redevelopment of specific large houses illustrates the larger schemes, but it was from the late 1970's that the process of converting large villas into upper and lower flats and building in the back or front gardens began to proliferate.

From the 1960's much new-build has taken place within the town and it is difficult to identify any one development which has added to the aesthetic value of the town, rather than detracting from what was an elegant community prior to the Second World War, the style of which had sustained its reputation.

If the reader has an interest in the old buildings in the area the bibliography records "'The North Clyde Estuary Architectural Guide" which was published in 1992 and is still in print at the time of writing. The author recommends this to any serious student of properties from Dumbarton through Cardross, up Loch Lomond side, round the Gareloch and over the Rosneath peninsular. All the properties are fully described, their history recorded and for most of them a photograph is in existence.

A significant development during the early 1980's was that area to the north of the railway station and bordering East King Street, which is currently occupied by a supermarket. Up to and including the 1970's this area was a goods yard with a spur line going behind the station and delivering goods and, in particular coal, into this area. In the earlier part of the 1900's, before road transport had been developed, this was the prime location for receiving goods of every description, but, as road transport took over, the area became largely disused in the late 1960's and 1970's. In the later period the area was used as an informal car park.

Prior the early 1980's the only supermarket was the small Tesco shop, formerly operated by William Low and Company on the right hand side of lower Sinclair Street. Most of the shopping for food was done in the myriad of local traders which served the town well for more that 100 years. With the advent of the major supermarket and the proliferation of cars from the 1960's onwards, which enabled people to visit Dumbarton or beyond, the locally-owned shops began to disappear. It was regrettable, as the local traders had provided an excellent service, including a comprehensive home-delivery system, for many decades.

Much of the development in the town from the 1950's onwards has taken place quietly and unobtrusively, small piece by small piece. One example was Waldie and Company, the original carter and garage in Helensburgh, whose premises had been reached through an archway to the south of Mackays stores at the foot of Sinclair Street. After the Second World War, one of the earliest petrol pumps was reached down this alleyway. A turntable is still in existence below the ground where the vehicle was filled up with petrol, the turntable revolved and the car drove out of the alleyway again. The alley has been converted into a shop, one of many such examples around the town

Up to 1953 local doctors consulted from their own homes. Dr. Harold Scott worked from his house at 11 Glennan Gardens. In that year Dr. Scott and his partners moved into an empty shop in Colquhoun Square, beside the West Kirk, which they had converted into consulting rooms. These premises are currently occupied by McArthur Stanton, solicitors. By the early 1970's the practice had moved to Scott Court in West Princes Street, and again a move to a purpose-built medical centre in East King Street was made in the mid-1990's

During the 1970's and early 1980's there was substantial development of the road system. In the early 1970's the only practical way to drive from Helensburgh towards Glasgow was to go through Cardross. At Dumbarton the only bridge was the old original one which led along the High Street and out onto the Glasgow road.

The new bridge, which now carries traffic straight through the middle of Dumbarton, bypassing the High Street, was completed in the mid 1970's.

Before development of the highways in the Vale of Leven, the road over the Black Hill, via Crosskeys, wound its way down and over an ancient bridge by Banachra. This route was superseded by a modern bridge which now takes traffic straight down to Arden roundabout, which was constructed in the late 1970's, replacing a T-junction, which had cottages on its left-hand corner.

The road towards Duck Bay and the Vale of Leven was widened and straightened, but prior to this it went immediately behind Cameron House Hotel and down to Balloch and onwards through Alexandria and Renton coming out towards Dumbarton. The current road, which takes you along the upper right hand side of the Vale of Leven as you travel towards Dumbarton, was only completed in the late 1970's and this development opened up the traffic route out of Helensburgh, via the Blackhill, which is now the common way of getting to the Glasgow area.

The substantial improvements to the road up Loch Lomondside to Tarbet were completed during the 1980's, forming the bypass to Luss which previously had to take all the traffic grinding its way through the village and past the Colquhoun Arms. A very substantial quantity of the rock which was blasted away to create this highway was tipped into a moss on the Loch Lomond golf course to create one of the holes. The rock had to fill a depth of 60 feet before it firmed out.

In the early 1970's a road was completed along the Gareloch, past Shandon and by-passing the Clyde Submarine Base. Even later in the late 1980's the road up to Whistlefield was completed, linking through again a new road over the hills to Coulport. Prior to this all the traffic had to go through Garelochhead, half way down Rosneath peninsular and over the hill which in bad weather became very difficult.

When the Faslane ship lift project and the development of Coulport was taking place during the mid 1980's, a large numbers of lorries had to travel past Helensburgh and a temporary service road was approved along the upper levels of Glen Fruin, on land leased from Luss Estates. However, in the early 1990's, when the construction traffic had finished, it became apparent that it was a useful addition to the road network and improvements were made to produce a long-term highway with permanent planning permission.

Developments have always taken place little by little and no doubt will continue to do so in the future. It is only possible to write down a snapshot of where we are and where we have come from. This book has attempted to cover the first two millennia and to record where we are as the third millennium starts.

BIBLIOGRAPHY

PRIME SOURCES

The book of Dumbarton, 3 volumes; Irvine 1879
Battrums Guide to Helensburgh; Battrum 1865
Annals of Garelochside; Maugham 1897
*Nonagenarians Reminiscences of Garelochside
And Helensburgh, and the people who dwelt within and
Therein;* McLeod 1883
The Story of Helensburgh; MacNeur and Brydon 1890
Helensburgh Guide Book; MacNeur and Brydon 1865
The statistical account of Scotland; First account 1791; Second
Account 1840; Third Account 1959
The History of Greenock; Murray Smith 1921
Helensburgh Directory; MacNeur and Brydon Annual 1865 – 1980
North Clyde Estuary – and illustrated architectural Guide;
Walker/Sinclair 1992
Short History of Dunbartonshire; MacPhail
*Helensburgh Town Council 1802 – 1975. A record of some of the
discussions of the council;* Norman Glen 1975
Historic Dumbarton – The Scottish Burgh Survey; Dennison/Coleman
1999

SECONDARY SOURCES

The travellers Guide Through Scotland, 1811 – The River Clyde; Reid
1886
The Beauties of Scotland; Vernon and Hood 1805
Helensburgh – The First Hundred Years; Laing 1985
Highland Heritage; Campbell 1962
New Ways Through the Glens; Haldane 1962
Tour of Scotch and English Lakes; Denholm 1804

Helensburgh Golf Club – A celebration of the first 100 years;
Helensburgh Golf Club 1993
100 Years of the West Highland Railway; McGregor 1994
The Clyde Submarine Base; Hall 1999
Clyde Shipwrecks; Crawford 1988
The Clyde River and Firth; Munro 1897

PICTORIAL SOURCES

The following are primarily pictorial records but all have
comprehensive notes of description.

Old Helensburgh, Rhu and Shandon; Hood 1999
Helensburgh in old picture postcards; Drayton 1985
Helensburgh in old picture postcards Vol. 1; Drayton 1985
Helensburgh in old picture postcards Vol. 2; Drayton 1986
Helensburgh Past and Present; Drayton 1999
Loch Lomond in Old Picture Postcards; Danielowski 1987
Glasgow Illustrated; Fairfield Smith 1999
The Clyde; Moss 1997
Greenock From Old Photographs; McCarroll 1983
The South Clyde Estuary, An Illustrated Architectural Guide; Walker
1986
Old Gourock; Twaddle 1999
Old Dumbarton; Hood 1999
Around Helensburgh; Helensburgh Heritage Trust 1999

Credit and thanks are due to the Helensburgh Library of Argyll and
Bute Council for permission to produce the photographs contained
in this book.